HOW

GROWS A

STRONG BOY

HOW
GOD
GROWS A
STRONG
BOY

A DEVOTIONAL

ELIJAH ADKINS

BARBOUR
kidz

Published by Barbour Publishing, Inc., 1810 Barbour Drive, Uhrichsville, Ohio 44683, www.barbourbooks.com

Our mission is to inspire the world with the life-changing message of the Bible.

Printed in China.
001757 1023 HA

INTRODUCTION

GOD IS GROWING YOU INTO A STRONG BOY!

"Be strong and have strength of heart. Do not be afraid or shake with fear because of them. For the Lord your God is the One Who goes with you. He will be faithful to you. He will not leave you alone."
DEUTERONOMY 31:6

God has big plans for you. And you can be confident in His plans because every day He is growing *you* into a strong boy. He will always be with you, and He will give you just the strength you need to choose faith over fear.

These devotions and prayers were written with you in mind. They are powerful reminders of the hope you have because you're God's boy. Touching on topics that matter to you, like family, friendships, trust, hope, and prayer, these readings will help you develop a deeper relationship with God as you grow into the strong boy He designed you to be.

With Him by your side, you can stand strong—no matter what.

IT'S YOUR TURN

*"Have I not told you? Be strong and have strength
of heart! Do not be afraid or lose faith. For the
Lord your God is with you anywhere you go."*
JOSHUA 1:9

Joshua had followed Moses—a strong, godly leader—for years. The journey had brought him through some fierce battles. He'd watched as enemies fell left and right—as God brought victory to his leader each time. But now Moses was gone, and Joshua needed to take his place.

Gulp.

What does that have to do with you? Well, every boy reaches a point when, like Joshua, he needs to make important decisions of his own. He has to take everything he's learned and decide how he's going to live his life.

Here's some great news: as long as you keep following God, He'll work powerfully in your life, slowly but surely forming you into the strong boy He intended you to be. So when that moment finally comes, you can stand up and say, "I'm ready, God!"

Now that's a cause for courage.

---

*Lord, I want to be strong when You call me—
just like Joshua. Keep teaching me each day so
I'll be prepared when the moment finally arrives.*

7

WAITING—NOT FOR THE WEAK

Wait for the Lord. Be strong. Let your heart
be strong. Yes, wait for the Lord.
PSALM 27:14

When you think of being strong, what comes to mind? A superhero flying through swarms of bad guys? A wrestler flexing his muscles?

Well, what about. . .waiting?

Imagine being in a room with a piece of candy. It's not your favorite, but hey—it's candy! Your parents say, "You can't eat that now. It'll spoil your appetite for dinner." Seconds tick by, then minutes, then hours. Soon, all you can think of is the candy across the room.

Finally, dinnertime arrives, and you devour everything on your plate. As you take your last bite, you see your mom take your favorite ice cream out of the freezer. Suddenly, that candy is the last thing on your mind—the ice cream is *so* much better.

God's promises are like that. Sometimes, you might get frustrated at God for asking you to wait for something. But as with that silly candy story, you'll soon learn that God has some great surprises awaiting.

Lord, give me the strength to wait. I know what
You have in store for me will be worth it.

NO FEAR HERE

"Do not be afraid. For I have bought you and made you free. I have called you by name. You are Mine!"
ISAIAH 43:1

Imagine trying to be perfect without God.

First, you'd have to stop sinning. . .for good. Second, you'd have to find a way to somehow get rid of all your past sins (time travel, maybe?). And then you'd have to learn literally everything all at once, just so you can always make the right decision at every point.

Ready? Okay, let's start in 3. . . 2. . . 1. . .

We're kidding, of course. Nobody could possibly do *any* of that. And even if you tried, you'd be paralyzed with fear for the rest of your life. One small mistake, and you'd be done for. How awful.

Thankfully, God knows this. That's why He sent Jesus—the only perfect Person in history—to take the punishment for our sins.

Now, there's no need to fear whenever you slip up. Instead, just ask God to forgive you. And just like that, your sin will be gone.

Thank You, Jesus, for making it possible for me to be forgiven. You're the only way I can be strong.

A DIFFERENT KIND OF HOPE

Be strong. Be strong in heart,
all you who hope in the Lord.
PSALM 31:24

Have you ever hoped for something good to happen? Maybe the teacher was calling out names for a group project, and you hoped you'd get paired with your best friend.

Sometimes, those hopes come true. Other times, reality is disappointing.

Thankfully, that kind of hope isn't the kind that today's verse is talking about. Hoping in the Lord isn't wishing for something; it's a solid confidence that God's promises will come to pass.

Imagine walking through a dark tunnel filled with snakes and deep pits, armed with nothing but that first kind of hope. Yikes! Well, now imagine walking through that same tunnel, but this time, you're right behind a grown-up with a flashlight.

Much better, right?

Thankfully, that's exactly the kind of hope God provides for His kids when life gets scary. Strong boys don't wish for something to happen—they put their hope in God.

God, I want my hope in You to be strong,
not wishy-washy or doubtful. That's the only
way I can be strong enough to face challenges.

FEAR—WHO NEEDS IT?

*For God did not give us a spirit of fear. He gave us
a spirit of power and of love and of a good mind.*
2 TIMOTHY 1:7

If anyone had a right to be afraid, it was the apostle Paul.
Many people tried telling him to pipe down about the
gospel, and when that didn't work, they tried to kill him.
In fact, when Paul wrote today's verse, he was in prison,
preparing to die for Jesus.

So how could this guy talk like everything was fine?
How could he teach the importance of fearlessness and
love and a "good mind"? Didn't he realize how bad his situation was?

Yes, he knew (see 2 Timothy 4:6). But he also knew
that the only thing those bad men could do was speed up
his trip to heaven. He didn't see that as much of a threat.

The next time you feel uncomfortable about sharing
the gospel with someone, remember Paul's example. With
God on his side, a strong boy has nothing to fear.

---

*Lord, I want to tell others about You. No matter
what happens, remind me that I have nothing
to fear—and every reason to be happy.*

THE BRIGHT SIDE

*"I have told you these things so you may have peace
in Me. In the world you will have much trouble.
But take hope! I have power over the world!"*
JOHN 16:33

Have you ever watched the news? If so, you probably saw a bunch of serious reporters showing videos of crime, talking about money problems, and going on about how we're all in so much trouble. Maybe there was a little nugget of good news somewhere in the middle, but then the bad stuff started back up again and drowned it all out.

No wonder some grown-ups are so depressed all the time.

Jesus knew all about this, so He gave His followers some important encouragement in today's verse. When life gets us down, we can be strong. Why? Because Jesus has "power over the world." Even if everything else goes wrong, there's one right thing that will stay right until the end of time—God's promise to lead His children home.

Now that's some good news.

---

*Lord Jesus, thank You for all the hope You bring.
Help me to always focus on the bright side of
things—because that's where You are.*

TRUE JOY

So we can say for sure, "The Lord is my Helper.
I am not afraid of anything man can do to me."
HEBREWS 13:6

Alex was an ordinary fifth grader. He had a few good friends, did well in his classes, and didn't have a lot of problems with bullies. Nothing too hard, but nothing too great either.

Then one Sunday at church, something strange happened. The preacher's words suddenly seemed real to him. Unable to explain this powerful new feeling, Alex accepted Jesus as his Savior.

The change was immediate. Each day, Alex woke up with a smile on his face and a song in his heart. But not everyone was as thrilled. Soon, some of his "friends" started making fun of him, calling him nasty names and mocking God.

But Alex didn't back down. His newfound happiness far outweighed any funny look or insult. Now that he'd found real joy, no bully could ever convince him to go back.

Lord, help me to stay strong, even when others
try to get me to go back. Nothing compares
to the great new life You've given me.

A PLACE TO STAND ON

This is the last thing I want to say:
Be strong with the Lord's strength.
EPHESIANS 6:10

Have you heard of Archimedes? He was an ancient Greek guy who is well known for his work on things like pulleys and levers. A lever is like a teeter-totter, but with a movable middle bar. If you move the bar (known as a "fulcrum") closer to a heavy object, you easily can lift that object by pulling down the long part of the teeter-totter. Archimedes supposedly said of the lever, "Give me a place to stand on, and I will move the earth."

You know what? God has given you a place to stand on—and it's Him. And using your faith in Him, like the bar of the lever, you can move the earth too. Or at least a mountain, like Jesus said (see Matthew 17:20).

Whenever you run into a big, heavy problem, you know that your own strength just won't cut it. But God's strength? It's more than enough.

God, help me always to trust in Your power instead of my own. That's the only way I'll ever be a strong boy.

MUCH-NEEDED SUPPORT

"But now be strong, Zerubbabel," says the Lord.
"Be strong, Joshua son of Jehozadak, head religious
leader. And be strong, all you people of the land,"
says the Lord. "Do the work, for I am with you."
HAGGAI 2:4

Jordan's knees were knocking as he got up to speak. He'd been chosen to recite the Gettysburg Address at a Memorial Day service, and he was scared. There were a lot more people in the audience than he expected, and he was sweating.

As he walked to the microphone, though, he noticed some movement in the back of the crowd. A man in Army fatigues was edging his way into the back seats—it was Jordan's dad! He'd been away in the service for months, and now here he was to support Jordan.

The boy took a deep breath, locked eyes with his dad, and started talking. And before he knew it, he was done. Everyone clapped, but there was a cheer from the back of the audience.

Isn't it great to know that whenever we get scared or nervous, God is watching us, cheering us on? With Him on our side, why would we ever feel afraid?

Thank You, God, for encouraging me when life gets
scary. With Your support, I know I'll be just fine.

CYCLE OF SUPPORT

Every one helps each other,
and says to his brother, "Be strong!"
ISAIAH 41:6

Have you ever hesitated to do something good—until your friend came along and convinced you with just a couple of words?

We all need those kinds of friends. They sometimes nudge us out of our comfort zones, challenging us to do the right thing when it isn't popular.

But have you ever thought that *you* can be that type of friend? Maybe a guy in your class is thinking about becoming a Christian. It's obvious that he's interested, but he's also scared about what others might think.

In that case, a simple "Be strong" might be all it takes. Once your friend knows he isn't alone, there will be nothing else to hold him back.

Often, God grows our strength so we can help grow the strength of others, who then help grow ours. That is so cool.

Lord, I want to encourage my friends to do the
right thing, just like You encourage me. Help me
to be that kind of friend to someone today.

THROUGH WATER AND FIRE

"When you pass through the rivers, they will not flow over you. When you walk through the fire, you will not be burned. The fire will not destroy you."
ISAIAH 43:2

Water and fire. What do those things have in common? If you answered, "They can both be dangerous," then you've gotten the point of today's verse.

Imagine walking through a river. You start off having fun, but before you know it your feet can't reach the bottom anymore and you start drifting away. Yikes!

Or think about campfires. They're great at taking the chill out of the air, but the moment you get too close . . .*ouch!* And don't even think about walking through it.

When God split the Red Sea wide open to let the Israelites pass through, and when He protected Shadrach, Meshach, and Abednego from the fiery furnace, He proved His power over the deepest of waters and the hottest of fires.

If God has so much power over nature, He's able to solve your problems.

God, I know that because You are strong, I can be strong too, no matter what comes my way.

STRONG THROUGH TEARS

You have seen how many places I have gone. Put my
tears in Your bottle. Are they not in Your book?
PSALM 56:8

Jonathan seemed fine to everyone else. He came to
school, told jokes with his friends, and then went home.
Perfectly normal, right?

Not exactly. Every day Jonathan came home, he
went to his room and cried. You see, Jonathan's dad had
passed away a year before that, and his mom had to work
long hours. He only got to see her for a few minutes each
day, and the babysitter didn't pay much attention to him
either.

How did Jonathan deal with such a sad situation? Well,
every time he started crying, he remembered today's
verse: "Put my tears in Your bottle." Over time, he felt
different. It was almost like somebody had whispered in
his ear, *I'm here.* Before long, his tears were drying. Sometimes, Jonathan even smiled. He knew God would stay by
his side, no matter how sad life got.

Lord Jesus, life can be really sad sometimes.
But I know You hear me when I'm down,
and that gives me a reason to be strong.

PEACE VS. PANIC

"Peace I leave with you. My peace I give to you.
I do not give peace to you as the world gives.
Do not let your hearts be troubled or afraid."
JOHN 14:27

Have you ever faced something scary—whether it was a hard test, a bully you see every day, or even moving to a new neighborhood—and you felt panicked? Of course. Everybody does. And if you're like most people, you probably whispered to yourself, "Stay calm."

That's easier said than done. Those two words alone won't give you a solid enough foundation to beat your fear—you have to have something more.

That's where Jesus comes in. Today's verse tells us we can beat fear by leaning on His promise to always be with us. No matter how scary life gets, His Holy Spirit will provide a way for us to be strong. All we have to do is ask.

How simple is that?

Thank You, Jesus, for providing a way to stay peaceful
when I panic. I'm so grateful to have You in my life.

ROLLING WITH THE PUNCHES

I can do all things because
Christ gives me the strength.
PHILIPPIANS 4:13

A lot of people see this verse and say something like, "Great! I'll run for president, and God will make sure I win." That's a really positive outlook, but it's not what this verse is talking about. Not even close.

In the previous verse, the apostle Paul spelled out exactly what he meant: "I know how to get along with little and how to live when I have much" (verse 12). This means God enabled us to be strong through both easy times (when we might be tempted to forget the Lord) and hard times (when we start wondering where God is). In other words, He gives us the ability to handle hardships.

This verse isn't magic you can use whenever you want something. If that were the case, many Christians around the world would be billionaires. Rather, it's a reminder that through thick and thin, God has your back.

Isn't that an even *better* promise?

Thank You, Lord, for promising to give me all I
need to stand strong when things get tough.

HOPELESS?

*Our hope comes from God. May He fill you with joy
and peace because of your trust in Him. May your
hope grow stronger by the power of the Holy Spirit.*
ROMANS 15:13

Have you ever messed up so badly—maybe on your
schoolwork, or at home, or in a friendship—that you lost
all hope for a happy ending? Knowing you've done something wrong, but being powerless to change it, is one of
the most terrible feelings in the world.

We understand the feeling because we've all hurt
someone we know. But have you ever stopped to think
that every sin you commit hurts God Himself? How on
earth can we make things up to Him?

That's where Jesus comes in. Because of His death on
the cross, our hopeless situations can be turned around
for good. Yes, we deserve punishment, but since Jesus already took that punishment, we can live forever with God.

Letting this truth sink deeply into your heart is an
important part of becoming a strong, hope-filled boy.

---

*Lord, I'm glad I don't have to be hopeless.
Instead, I can walk through life strong and
secure. Thank You for this fantastic gift.*

SEARCHING FOR STRENGTH

I looked for the Lord, and He answered me.
And He took away all my fears.
PSALM 34:4

People look for strength in some pretty messed-up places. Some think making other people feel bad will somehow boost their own self-esteem—so they become bullies. Some feel weak by themselves, so they hang around bad people who encourage them to do evil. Some even turn to alcohol or drugs to give them a "rush" of power—though it doesn't take long before those things take over.

There's got to be a better way, right?

Yes! Today's verse points to the only way a boy can truly become strong: God. Without God, life is just empty and sad. But as long as you know God is with you, helping you along through the confusing parts of life, you have all the strength you need.

The search stops with Him.

Lord God, I'm glad I don't have to search
for power in all the wrong places. Thank You
for giving me all the strength I need.

PATIENCE, PATIENCE

*God has chosen you. You are holy and loved by Him.
Because of this, your new life should be full of loving-pity.
You should be. . .gentle and be willing to wait for others.*
COLOSSIANS 3:12

Kyle was getting impatient. The new kid—Jason was his name—just never stopped talking. Jason didn't have many friends besides Kyle. So everything that was on his mind usually went into Kyle's ears. Didn't he know Kyle was busy?

But suddenly, Kyle remembered something. A couple of years earlier, he had been the new kid at school. He had made only a couple of friends right away, but those friends had been really nice to him. And if he was being honest, Kyle had to admit that he'd been something of a chatterbox himself. Where would he be now if his friends had just walked away?

Kyle took a deep breath and leaned against the hallway wall. "So, then what happened?" he asked—and then actually listened to Jason's reply.

---

*Lord, I know You've been unbelievably patient
with me. Please give me the strength to be patient
with others too, even when they seem annoying.*

23

PAIN HURTS

The little troubles we suffer now for a short time are making us ready for the great things God is going to give us forever.
2 CORINTHIANS 4:17

Nobody likes going to the dentist. It takes time, it's kind of awkward, and—depending on the reason for your visit—it can *hurt*.

But imagine a world where everybody stopped going to the dentist. Healthy, shiny teeth would soon disappear—and many people might lose their teeth altogether. Clearly, a little pain or discomfort here and there is worth the trouble of a healthy mouth.

The trials we face in this life are like trips to the dentist. They're often sad and painful—if not physically, then emotionally. And sometimes, they may hurt a lot more than any dentist drill ever could.

But if shiny teeth sound like a great reward for going to the dentist, just think of the reward for staying faithful to God—eternal life with Him.

Pain hurts, God. But because You've promised me heaven, I know I can be strong, even in the moments I'm hurting the most. Thank You for such an awesome reward.

EMERGENCY

You answered me on the day I called.
You gave me strength in my soul.
PSALM 138:3

When Jordan went hiking with his friend Albert behind his house, he was expecting a fun, problem-free adventure. But about an hour into the walk, something horrible happened: Albert tripped and hit his head. At first, Jordan thought he was playing, but after a few seconds of Albert laying still, Jordan started to panic. *What do I do?*

Then he remembered the cellphone his mom had handed him just before he left. With trembling fingers, he dialed 911 and told the dispatcher the problem. Medics soon arrived, loading poor Albert onto a stretcher.

Good news: Albert turned out just fine.

With three taps on a phone, Jordan had access to trained emergency help. But think about this: you can call the best Doctor in the universe with a single word. No matter what your emergency, call out to the one who made you. God is always listening, always waiting to answer.

Lord, I know You're always available, even when I don't have time for a long, fancy prayer. Because of that, I know I can be strong, no matter how scary life gets.

STRENGTH TO SHARE

"For we must tell what we have seen and heard."
ACTS 4:20

It's sad but true: most people just don't like hearing the gospel these days. Telling others about Jesus isn't exactly a crime—like it was in Peter and John's day—but it's becoming less and less accepted by many.

But people's negative reactions don't make the message untrue. It's the most important message of all! And guess who God wants to tell others about Him? Yep—people like you.

Sure, it'll probably be awkward. But God doesn't just leave us by ourselves. He promises to be with us as we spread His Word, even to the end of time (Matthew 28:20).

So today, why not be strong by sharing the love of Jesus with someone who really needs it? You—and perhaps the person you're talking to—will be glad you did.

---

*Lord Jesus, after all You've done for me, the least
I can do is tell other people. Give me the strength
to share Your good news with friends, family,
classmates, and everyone else I meet.*

HARD CHOICES

"I will go in to the king,
which is against the law."
ESTHER 4:16

Esther isn't just a girl's book. The fact is, boys can learn a lot from her courage.

In the story, an evil man named Haman had convinced the king to sign a law that would kill all the Jews in Persia. The king's wife, Esther, had a big problem—she was Jewish, though she'd never told the king about it. She couldn't just stand by and watch this happen to her people.

But there was *another* problem—if Esther approached the king unannounced, he could have her killed. So what did Esther do? She gritted her teeth, straightened her spine, and said, "If I die, I die." Then she went straight to the king.

Thankfully, the king was happy to see her. She convinced him to save her people.

Not all of us have the chance to be as heroic as Esther. But each day we're presented with many opportunities to stand up for what's right. What will you do with those chances?

Lord, I want to stand up for You, even if
it means other kids will make fun of me.
Give me the strength to be like Esther.

GREAT EXAMPLES

Then David said to his son Solomon,
"Be strong. . . . Do not be afraid or troubled,
for the Lord God, my God, is with you."
1 CHRONICLES 28:20

If anyone knew what it meant to be strong, it was David. Throughout his life, he'd been through just about everything—wild animals attacking his sheep, a battle against a giant warrior, an evil king trying to kill him, and his own son trying to take his crown. Each trial seemed worse than the last, but each time, David walked out unharmed. How? Because he knew God was with him.

Now it was time for David's son Solomon to take his place as king. Knowing that Solomon had the huge responsibility of building God's temple, David gave him the only advice he knew: trust God. Solomon knew David's words were true—the evidence was David himself.

Who can you look up to as proof of God's guidance and protection?

Thank You, Lord, for not only promising to be
with me but giving me examples to back up Your
promise. Give me the strength to follow these
examples whenever it's my turn to be strong.

GOD'S STAMP OF APPROVAL

Then Peter and the missionaries said,
"We must obey God instead of men!"
ACTS 5:29

One day, Gregory was walking from the bus to the school when he saw a group of his friends gathered around the back of the building, snickering. He jogged over to them.

"Hey, Greg," said Will, the unofficial leader of the group. "We were just waiting for you to join in on the fun."

Gregory turned around and gasped. A string of really nasty words was spray painted across the side of the building, and now Will was handing over the spray can.

Gregory paused to think, then put up his hand. "No thanks. I don't think God—or my teachers and parents— would like it if I did that."

Will smirked and called Gregory a wimp. But as Gregory walked away, he felt only relief. He may have lost a friend or two, but he'd gained something more important: God's approval.

What could ever top that?

Lord Jesus, I want to obey You rather than other
people. I know that when a "friend" tries to get me
to disobey You, he isn't a friend worth keeping anyway.

WHEN GRATITUDE GETS TOUGH

*In everything give thanks. This is what God
wants you to do because of Christ Jesus.*
1 THESSALONIANS 5:18

Some boys grow up with super-rich parents. They have expensive houses, fancy clothes, and tons of video games. Maybe you're one of those boys.

More than likely, however, you can't relate to any of that. If so, that's okay. In fact, that's great. Jesus Himself talked about how easy it is for rich people to miss what really matters (Matthew 19:24).

But what about if you're the *opposite* of rich? What if your parents can hardly afford groceries, let alone cool cars and fancy televisions?

Believe it or not, the Bible says you should be thankful for that too. It's easy to be grateful when everything is going your way, but when things get tough, it takes strength to say, "Thank You, God, for the blessings I do have."

Keeping a thankful spirit helps you to trust God through anything life throws at you.

---

*Father, I may not be rich, but I have all that
matters—the promise of eternal life with You.
Thank You for this amazing treasure.*

HAPPY ENDINGS

*"For I know the plans I have for you," says
the Lord, "plans for well-being and not for
trouble, to give you a future and a hope."*
JEREMIAH 29:11

When was the last time you watched a really suspenseful movie? Maybe the good guy was on the run from some really bad dudes. But just when all hope seemed lost, the odds flipped. The good guy finally won.

Today's verse is useful for those times when *we* feel like the main character of a suspense movie—scared, hopeless, and on the run. Life can be tough, so this feeling is a lot more common than you'd think.

Not only is the Lord there to walk with you when you're overwhelmed—He also promises that the ending to your story has already been written. And guess what? As long as you're one of His kids, that ending will be better than any "happily ever after" that Hollywood could dream up.

---

*Lord God, I know that because You've written
a happy ending to my story, I can be strong,
even when disaster is right on my tail.*

GOD'S GOT YOU SURROUNDED

*Where can I go from Your Spirit? Or where can I run
away from where You are? If I go up to heaven, You
are there! If I make my bed in the place of the dead,
You are there! If I take the wings of the morning or
live in the farthest part of the sea, even there Your
hand will lead me and Your right hand will hold me.*
PSALM 139:7–10

It's impossible to hide from God. You can run a couple of
blocks across town, or jump in a car to speed to another
state. You could even blast off in a rocket ship to the
moon. But wherever you go, God will be just as close to
you as He was the moment you left.

He's everywhere, and He's not going anywhere.

Of course, this is bad news for people who want to
hide their sin. But for those boys who are trying to stay
strong, even when they're scared, sad, or alone, it's the
greatest news in the universe.

So stay strong—God's got you surrounded.

---

*Thank You, Father, for surrounding me at all times,
even when it doesn't feel like You're there.*

SHATTERED HEARTS

Those who are right with the Lord cry, and He hears
them. And He takes them from all their troubles.
The Lord is near to those who have a broken heart.
And He saves those who are broken in spirit.
PSALM 34:17–18

Having a broken heart is never fun. In fact, it's one of the worst feelings in the world. When the thing you've hoped for the most falls apart in front of you, it can feel like your heart has shattered into a million tiny pieces.

But did you know that your broken heart is the perfect place for God to start working?

You see, it's really easy to get attached to the things of this world—so attached that we lose sight of what truly matters. Sometimes God uses our disappointments to tear down our ideas of what we think life should be. Then He replaces those wrong ideas with what He knows is best.

When life is at its lowest, strong boys look up.

Thank You, Lord, for breaking my heart every
now and then. Keep working on me until I
become the man You've made me to be.

TOO FAST

*Our life is lived by faith. We do not
live by what we see in front of us.*
2 CORINTHIANS 5:7

Over 210 miles per hour. That's how fast Dan Parker's car was going when he shattered the world record.

Pretty impressive, you may think, *but haven't other people gone faster?* Of course they have. But Dan is blind.

Yes, you read that right. A blind man driving 210 mph! How in the world did he do that? He can't even see what's in front of him. Well, he didn't have to. While Dan was racing down a runway, the car's computer guided him with unique sounds. He may have been blind, but he could still hear.

That's what today's verse means for us. We can't always see what's ahead in life. That's why a strong boy learns to listen to God's Spirit. The Lord guides us where we need to go—whispering directions and advice. All we need to do is pay attention.

---

*God, I thank You for Your Spirit. With Your help,
I can keep pressing forward, unconcerned
about what might lie ahead.*

SCARY STORMS

But the Lord has been my strong place,
my God, and the rock where I am safe.
PSALM 94:22

Jimmy and his family crouched in their dark basement, listening to the tornado sirens blaring in the distance. Then he started hearing *other*, far scarier sounds coming from above. Crunching, smashing, ripping, shaking, and then. . .silence.

After a few minutes, Jimmy's dad slowly opened the basement door—only to find the whole house above them completely gone. The family tearfully hugged each other, grateful to be alive. Jimmy realized that was all that mattered.

Sometimes, the things we go through can feel like a tornado. Unfair—even tragic—things happen all the time, tearing down our plans and threatening to blow away our courage. But during these times, God is like a stormproof basement. Sure, we'll be afraid. We might even lose a lot. But when the storm is over, we'll find that everything we need is safe with Him.

Thank You, God, for promising to protect
me when I'm scared and uncertain. Help me
run to You whenever I need strength.

DISASTER

*God is our. . .help when we are in trouble. So we will not
be afraid, even if the earth is shaken and the mountains
fall into the center of the sea, and even if its waters go
wild with storm and the mountains shake with its action.*
PSALM 46:1–3

Have you ever seen a disaster movie? If so, maybe you
thought of that when you read today's verses. Mountain-
breaking earthquakes? Check. Huge tidal waves? Yes.
End-of-the-world chaos? You bet!

In fact, it's pretty hard to get any more extreme than
this scripture. But that's what makes the author's words
even more amazing: "We will not be afraid." Wow! God is
so strong—so big and powerful—that even the worst-case
scenario is not a problem.

And if God can handle all that, think of how easy it
is for Him to take care of the issues you face each day.
Tough classes at school, tests, bullies; none of them are a
problem for God.

If that's not a reason to be strong, what is?

---

*Life is stressful sometimes, Lord. When I get scared,
remind me that You've got everything under control.*

PRISON PRAISE

*Be happy in your hope. Do not give up when trouble
comes. Do not let anything stop you from praying.*
ROMANS 12:12

Paul and Silas weren't having the best of days. Having
been thrown in jail for preaching about Jesus, they had
every reason to start singing sad songs.

Well, they *did* start singing—praises to God, that is
(Acts 16:25).

More than likely, you won't be beaten or thrown in
jail for telling your friends about Jesus. But what if they
make fun of you and call you names? What if they try their
hardest to get you in trouble?

Maybe you've already gone through something like
that. If so, don't worry. Jesus Himself said that because
the world hated Him, it will naturally hate anyone who
follows Him (John 15:18). But here's the good news—Jesus
has power over the world (John 16:33).

So what do you do "when trouble comes"? Put on a
smile and keep on praying. That will make and keep you
strong.

---

*Lord Jesus, help me to follow Your example and
keep doing what's right, even if it's unpopular.*

WHOSE SIDE ARE YOU ON?

What can we say about all these things?
Since God is for us, who can be against us?
ROMANS 8:31

Gideon lived long before today's verse was even written, yet he understood its meaning more than most of us could today.

With nothing but three hundred guys, a few torches and trumpets, and a calling from God, Gideon faced off against a huge enemy army. But the only thing that really mattered was that calling.

Because God was on his side, Gideon's enemies didn't stand a chance.

Maybe you're facing a scary challenge, wondering how you're going to come out on top. Well, here's the short answer: you won't. Not by yourself, anyway. But if God is on your side, the odds are suddenly in your favor.

To become a strong boy, make sure your goals match up with God's. If they do, what could possibly stand in your way?

Thank You, God, for promising to fight for me. Help me always stay inside Your plan. That way, I won't have to rely on my own strength but on Yours instead.

"ALL" MEANS "ALL"

"For God can do all things."
LUKE 1:37

This little statement covers so much that we'd be foolish to try to understand it all.

What does "all things" mean? For the answer, look no further than the miracles of the Bible. Seas split down the middle, people walking on water, storms disappearing, and the dead getting up and walking. When God says *all* things, He's not bluffing.

Right now, you're still young, so your experience with God's power might be limited. Maybe He's guided you through a test at school, helped you tell a hard truth to your parents, or given you the right words when sharing the gospel.

As you grow older, though, this list will expand. Eventually, it'll be so big that whenever the next scary challenge comes up, you'll just add it to the list and thank God for answering your prayer.

That's what true faith is all about: remembering that with God, "all" means "all."

---

*Lord, help me to remember that there's no limit
to Your power, even when I don't see a way out.*

IS THAT ALL YOU GOT?

When I am afraid, I will trust in You. I praise the Word of God. I have put my trust in God. I will not be afraid. What can only a man do to me?
PSALM 56:3–4

When it comes to growing into a strong boy, this verse is like Basic Training. Not only does it give you a response to every scary situation—it also tells you to ask a simple question that will set your mind on track: "What can only a man do to me?"

In reality, you can replace the word *man* with just about anything. Whether it's something as serious as a bad sickness or as minor as a bad thunderstorm, nothing is too hard for God to take care of. And because you're God's kid, even death itself is nothing but a small step into your forever home with Him.

When life gets out of control, a strong boy can look fear straight in the eyes and say, "Is that all you've got?"

Thank You, Lord, for being stronger than all my fears.

NIGHT OF THE MUMMY

"Gather together riches in heaven where they will not be eaten by bugs or become rusted. Men cannot break in and steal them. For wherever your riches are, your heart will be there also."
MATTHEW 6:20–21

In ancient Egypt, rulers were buried with tons of gold and expensive treasures. They hoped that when they woke up in the afterlife, all this treasure would be theirs forever.

Good luck with that!

Everything decays with time. Grave robbers have stolen many treasures from tombs. Sand and bugs and who knows what else have filled those once impressive tombs. Only a fraction of the treasures remain today. And even if all of it were untouched, how much of it would those mummified kings would be enjoying right now, anyway?

But if you're chuckling at those silly Egyptian kings, ask yourself if you're doing the same thing. Often, we get so excited about money and useless gadgets that we lose sight of the one thing that will truly last forever: our relationship with God.

Strong boys realize that just like the mummy's treasure, nothing on earth will do us any good once we're gone.

Lord, thank You for giving me a hope that lasts forever.

HIDDEN PURPOSE

Be quiet and know that I am God.
I will be honored among the nations.
I will be honored in the earth.
PSALM 46:10

Have you ever been upset over God's way of doing things? Maybe you really hoped to get a spot on the team, but another kid won it instead. Or maybe you had to say goodbye to your best friend as he moved out of state. Either way, you find yourself saying, "Lord, was that really necessary?"

And you know what His answer is? *Yes.* Nothing happens that God doesn't have a reason for. Maybe that kid who got your spot has been praying for it longer than you have. And maybe there are some non-Christians in that other town who need to see the love your friend has to show.

Strong boys remember that life may not always go the way they want. But everything is working toward God's glory. If you're one of His kids, that should be the greatest news in the world.

Lord, I want everything that happens to honor You.
Help me to trust that You know exactly what You're doing.

GOD STICKS AROUND

You must keep praying. Keep watching!
Be thankful always.
COLOSSIANS 4:2

Have you ever felt like God didn't hear your prayers? Like no matter how much you talked to God, He wasn't even listening?

Don't worry—you're not alone. The great prophet Elijah once felt completely abandoned, so much so that he wanted to die (1 Kings 19). David wrote several psalms about how lonely and defeated he felt. Even Jesus cried out on the cross, "My God, My God, why have You left Me alone?" (Matthew 27:46). But in each of these cases, God came through just in time.

Strong boys realize that God always sticks around, even when we don't feel like He's there. If you're feeling alone, then pray. If you're feeling knocked down and sad, pray. If you're feeling all dried up inside, pray.

Keep praying and thanking God for working in your life. You never know when He'll step in and change everything.

Thank You, Lord, for working behind the scenes
and staying by my side. When I feel alone,
help me to remember that You're always there.

IN GOOD HANDS

The Lord said, "I Myself will go
with you. I will give you rest."
EXODUS 33:14

Have you ever worked so hard on something that you felt like you couldn't do anything else? Maybe you and your family were cleaning out a room, and you found yourself carrying something that was way too heavy. You felt it slipping from your hands as you walked. Your arms ached, and it felt like your shoulders were about to pop out of joint. Suddenly, your dad saw you struggling, and *swoop!*— just like that, he scooped it out of your hands and carried it for you. You collapsed on the couch, exhausted and thankful for some much-needed rest.

That's exactly what this verse says God does for us. Trying to live the Christian life in our own power just makes us tired and frustrated. But when we let God snatch the worry, fear, and stress out of our grip, we can rest in His love. Our problems are in good hands.

Lord, I'm glad I don't have to carry all my
problems alone. Thank You for Your rest.

LOOKS DON'T MATTER

"A man looks at the outside of a person,
but the Lord looks at the heart."
1 Samuel 16:7

Nobody liked Jenny, the new kid at school. She was quiet and kept to herself. Maybe it was because of the hunch in her back and the awkward way she walked around. Pretty much everyone—including Caleb, the "popular guy"—thought she was strange.

One day, Caleb and Jenny were assigned to the same project. At first, Caleb was unhappy. But over the next few days, he began to realize that Jenny was actually pretty cool.

Born with some physical challenges, Jenny had heard hundreds of insults over the years. Eventually, she'd just stopped talking entirely. But as Caleb opened up to her, Jenny started opening up as well. And as it turns out, she was one of the nicest people he'd ever met.

Caleb soon apologized for the hurtful things he'd said, and he stood up for her every time someone else insulted her.

Caleb had discovered the true meaning of today's verse—and for the first time in his life, he had a true friend.

Help me, God, to see others the way You see them—
to look past appearances and into the heart.

STRONGER THAN STRONG

For I know that nothing can keep us from the love of God.
Death cannot! Life cannot! Angels cannot! Leaders cannot!
Any other power cannot! Hard things now or in the future
cannot! The world above or the world below cannot! Any
other living thing cannot keep us away from the love
of God which is ours through Christ Jesus our Lord.
ROMANS 8:38–39

What's the strongest substance in the world? Believe it or not, it isn't diamond. Instead, it's something called graphene. As one professor put it, "It would take an elephant, balanced on a pencil, to break through a sheet of graphene the thickness of Saran Wrap."

But you know what's even more powerful than graphene? That's right—God's love. God loves you so much that nothing can pry Him away from you. Not the sharpest knife or the heaviest jackhammer or even the biggest elephant standing on the thinnest pencil could poke through His love.

Since God's love is so strong, you can be strong too.

Lord, my mind can't grasp how powerful Your
love is. Thank You for this amazing gift.

IT'S A GOOD DAY

This is the day that the Lord has made.
Let us be full of joy and be glad in it.
PSALM 118:24

We all know God never makes mistakes. If He did, He wouldn't be God anymore. But what does this have to do with today's verse?

It's simple: if today's the day the Lord has made, then it *must* be good. Otherwise, God wouldn't have made it.

But wait, you may think, *I had a bad time at school today. Everyone's been grumpy with me. I even tripped and scraped my knee. What's so good about that?*

Well, something can be good overall even if not every part is wonderful by itself. You wouldn't want to eat all the ingredients of a cake by themselves, would you?

The Bible says that God can take evil things and turns them into good (Genesis 50:20). He can use what seem to be sloppy drops of paint to create a fantastic work of art.

This is the day God has made for you. Rejoice and be glad in it!

Lord, when I'm down, please give me a glimpse of the bigger picture You're painting. I know that no matter how things look now, the end result will be beautiful.

GOD'S "PARADOX"

*The peace of God is much greater than the human
mind can understand. This peace will keep your
hearts and minds through Christ Jesus.*
PHILIPPIANS 4:7

Do you know what a paradox is? To put it simply, it's two statements that seem to contradict each other while being true at the same time.

God really loves paradoxes. In order to live forever, you first have to die to yourself. To be first, you've got to be last. And, to bring it back to today's verse, God's peace is strongest in the middle of a storm.

How is that possible? Doesn't peace mean nothing bad is happening? Nope. Peace isn't about what's happening around you; it's about what's happening *inside* you. You can be in the middle of the biggest hurricane the world has ever seen, but if you trust God enough, your soul will be as peaceful as a smooth, quiet pond.

Sometimes the only way a boy can become strong is by leaning on God through the rough spots in life. Are you ready to live God's paradox?

---

*Lord, I know I don't have things under control.
But that's okay—I know You do.*

DOUBT YOUR DOUBTS

Jesus said, "Come!" Peter got out of the
boat and walked on the water to Jesus.
MATTHEW 14:29

Peter was a fisherman, so he was pretty familiar with water. He knew that when it was calm, the surface was beautiful and the fish below were just waiting to be caught. Peter also knew that when a storm came, that water could turn into something terrifying and deadly.

But for all his time on the water, Peter had yet to see one thing: somebody walking on it. So when he saw Jesus stepping across the waves—and inviting Peter to step out too—he was terrified. But he obeyed—and he made it pretty far, all things considered.

Sometimes God challenges us to look again at situations we think we understand. Even if you've been disappointed in the past and expect nothing greater out of the future, God still calls you to doubt your doubts. You never know when a miracle is right around the corner.

Thank You for being a God of miracles. I know
that with You, I always have hope for tomorrow,
no matter how bad things may look now.

EASY LOAD

*"Come to Me, all of you who work and have heavy
loads. I will give you rest. Follow My teachings and
learn from Me. I am gentle and do not have pride.
You will have rest for your souls. For My way of
carrying a load is easy and My load is not heavy."*
MATTHEW 11:28–30

A lot of people don't want to be Christian because they
hate the thought of following rules. What they don't
realize, though, is that the Bible isn't all about rules—its
about a personal relationship with Jesus. All those "rules"
are simply descriptions of how a true Christian will *want*
to act. If we fail and say we're sorry, Jesus says, "Forgiven."

Not only does being a Christian give you hope and
joy, but the Holy Spirit inside you changes your desires
to match up with God's. As a result, the more a boy relies
on God's strength to change him, the stronger he himself
will become.

Now isn't that easy?

---

*Thank You, God, for making
it so easy to put my trust in You.*

NO NEED TO RUSH

I wait for the Lord. My soul
waits and I hope in His Word.
PSALM 130:5

Do you sometimes get tired of waiting? Maybe you feel like you're ready to be a teenager—to have more freedom to do what you want. But once you reach that age, you'll find yourself impatient for your driver's license. And once that happens, you'll want to be an adult. And then you might wait to find a good job. . .to get married. . .to buy a better house. . .and on and on it goes.

The point is this: if you spend your life impatient for the next big thing, you'll miss all the smaller blessings that life is really made of.

Trusting God's timing is an important part of becoming a strong boy. When you do, you'll not only grow in faith but also find yourself free to enjoy life as it happens.

There's no need to rush.

Thank You, Lord, for having the future already
figured out. Help me to be patient for every
blessing, even the ones that feel overdue.

X MARKS THE SPOT

*And my God will give you everything you need
because of His great riches in Christ Jesus.*
PHILIPPIANS 4:19

Imagine you're in the back yard, and you notice a strange mark on the ground. Curious, you grab a shovel and start digging a hole. Then, suddenly—*clunk!*

Your curiosity changes to excitement as you scoop out a small metal box. It's crazy heavy, and when you open it you see hundreds of gold coins. You're suddenly a millionaire!

Strangely enough, you notice some shiny, gold letters on the back of the chest—it's your own name.

Sure, this story is pretty unlikely to happen. But think of this: the day you asked Jesus to come into your heart, you received a treasure so big that it makes a chest full of gold seem like a few pennies and a couple of bottlecaps. Because unlike this make-believe treasure chest, *God's treasure will last forever.*

---

*Lord, whenever I start feeling down, remind me how
great of a treasure I have in my heart. This amazing
truth will give me the strength to get through anything.*

WORRISOME WORRIES

Do not worry. Learn to pray about everything.
Give thanks to God as you ask Him for what you need.
PHILIPPIANS 4:6

Do you know someone who's always worried about things? Even when it's sunny and clear outside, he stays inside wondering, *But what if it storms?*

Some people's worries are so extreme sometimes that it's easy to laugh. But don't we all do the same thing at times?

God has done so much to prove how powerful and good He is, so it should be foolish for us to worry about anything. And yet every time a minor problem pops up, we worry.

That's where today's verse comes in. Every time you notice worry in your gut—that awful feeling that you *know* something bad is going to happen—try putting the feeling into words. Speak it to God. Then thank Him ahead of time for His answer.

Overcoming worry is a great way for a strong boy to get even stronger.

Thank You, God, for giving me a reason not to worry.
Help me trust You whenever I get scared.

ABOVE THE CLOUDS

*The Lord God is my strength. He has made
my feet like the feet of a deer, and He
makes me walk on high places.*
HABAKKUK 3:19

Some people are scared of heights. They decide to ride a
roller coaster, only to find they've made a *big* mistake. Or
maybe they have to walk across a really high bridge, and
feel their legs getting wobbly as they glance over the side.

In life, each of us has a "high place" that we have
to deal with. When the future is scary and things have a
chance to go badly, we can feel like we're standing on
the edge of a high cliff, even above the clouds. Habakkuk
certainly knew what that felt like—but he also knew that
with God by his side, a fear of heights just doesn't apply.
Even if he took the plunge, he knew God was strong
enough to give him wings.

Now *that's* what it means to be fearless.

---

*Help me, Lord, to be strong enough to trust You,
even when I'm out of my comfort zone.*

HIDE AND SEEK

*"You will look for Me and find Me,
when you look for Me with all your heart."*
JEREMIAH 29:13

Hide and seek is probably one of the most popular games ever. You've probably played it many times with your friends or brothers or sisters. It's fun to try to find where another person is hiding. It's also a great way to train your brain to be more attentive.

The more you look, the better you'll become at noticing small details—that little crack between those drawers . . .that area behind the laundry baskets. . .and how much space there was under the bed.

Looking for God can work the same way. If God just gave us everything right away, we'd get lazy pretty fast. But the way God grows a strong boy's curiosity is by hiding Himself within His Word. That way, if we want to know more about Him, then all we have to do is open the Bible and start looking. And the more we search, the better we'll become at digging even deeper.

Lord, help me to never lose interest in searching for You.

SEEING A BIG GOD WITH TINY EYES

*"For as the heavens are higher than the earth,
so are My ways higher than your ways, and
My thoughts than your thoughts."*
Isaiah 55:9

One day, Silas noticed something sad: a tiny fly was struggling in the pool, sending out tiny ripples in the water.

So Silas scooped the fly out of the water and put him on dry land. Just then, a thought passed through his head: *What does that fly think of me?* Maybe the fly saw Silas coming and got scared. Or maybe the fly didn't notice Silas at all—the boy was just too big for its tiny eyes to see.

Compared to God, each person is like that fly. Because God is so big, it's hard for us to wrap our mind around Him. So some people get scared of Him. Others don't even seem to notice Him.

God's kids, however, know enough—what the Bible tells us about God. Strong boys know that He's real and that He loves us more than we could ever understand.

Lord, the only way I can be strong is to realize how strong You are. Without You, I'd be just a fly in the water.

DESERT PARADISE

But I am like a green olive tree in the house of God.
I trust in the loving-kindness of God forever and ever.
PSALM 52:8

Imagine a world like the kind you'd see in a scary sci-fi movie. Everything's a hot, barren desert. Dust swirls around where life used to exist. Animal skeletons lie scattered everywhere, and the remains of skyscrapers are toppled in the sand.

Then imagine that, right in the middle of all this, is a single house. And within that house is a beautiful green tree with hundreds of olives hanging from its branches.

As it turns out, that's a perfect description of what happens when a boy puts his trust in God. The world doesn't have much to offer when it comes to spiritual food. It's about as dead as dead can get. But thanks to God, your spirit can grow and rejoice as long as you stick by His side.

And no amount of dust and dryness can stop that.

Thank You, God, for giving me a paradise in the middle of the desert. Help me continue growing until I'm a strong tree within Your house.

LOST IN THE WOODS

Trust in the Lord with all your heart, and do not trust in your own understanding. Agree with Him in all your ways, and He will make your paths straight.
PROVERBS 3:5–6

"If you ever get lost, just follow these orange markings on the trees. They'll lead you straight down to the camp."

The words of Robby's youth camp instructor rattled in his head as he stumbled through the weeds in the increasing darkness. He'd heard about bears that roamed these woods at night.

It took Robby a couple of minutes to find the first marking—a little orange arrow painted on the side of an old oak tree. Sure enough, before long, he found himself at the bottom of the mountain where a group of his friends were waiting.

When life gets confusing—when you feel like Robby in the woods—turn to the Bible for direction. As long as you're following God, even the most crooked of paths will suddenly become straight as an arrow.

Help me be strong enough to search for Your signal, God, whenever I get lost. Show me the way back home.

WITH FLYING COLORS

*My Christian brothers, you should be happy
when you have all kinds of tests. You know these
prove your faith. It helps you not to give up.*
JAMES 1:2–3

Brandon stared at the test sheet. He'd studied hard the night before, and he remembered reading about almost every question on the page, but the answers just wouldn't come. This was going to be *bad*.

Suddenly, he heard the teacher say: "And don't forget, class. This test is open book."

Just like that, Brandon's grimace turned into a grin. He scooped his textbook out of his bookbag and flipped to the right chapter. The answers were all in here, and he knew *exactly* where to find them.

When life throws you a test and it's hard to stay strong or tell right from wrong, remember: this test is open book. The book, of course, is the Bible. And as long as you remember to use it, you'll find yourself smiling every time a test arrives—because you know you can pass it with flying colors.

---

*Thank You, Lord, for making life an open book test.
Remind me to read this book—Your Word—every day.*

WHAT'S ON THE INSIDE

*Your beauty should come from the inside. It should come
from the heart. This is the kind that lasts. Your beauty
should be a gentle and quiet spirit. In God's sight this is
of great worth and no amount of money can buy it.*
1 PETER 3:4

Ew! you may be thinking. *This is a book for boys! What's a
verse about beauty doing in here?*

Well, today's verse does speak to women. But it's a
message about much more than just the way someone
looks. Peter was talking about what goes on inside a person's heart—and that's for both girls and guys. God doesn't
care about looks. He's much more interested in our loyalty
and humility when it comes to serving Him.

So you can replace the word *beauty* with *strength* if
you'd like, and the verse works just as well. As long as your
soul lines up the way God wants, it doesn't matter how big
your muscles are. God sees you as one of His kids, and that
gives you all the strength you'll ever need.

---

*Lord, I want my soul, not my body, to be my
priority. Teach me how to stay spiritually fit.*

BEFORE/AFTER

*He answered me, "I am all you need. I give
you My loving-favor. My power works best in
weak people." I am happy to be weak and have
troubles so I can have Christ's power in me.*
2 CORINTHIANS 12:9

Have you ever seen a before-and-after picture on an ad
for exercise equipment? Maybe you've noticed that the
"before" side features a skinny guy who looks like he
couldn't lift ten pounds, but then the "after" side shows
the Incredible Hulk (minus the green).

Now imagine if that guy in the "before" picture looked
just as pumped up as the second one. Would you be as im-
pressed? No, because the entire point of the commercial
was to make you say, "Wow! What a change!"

That's the point of today's verse too. Each one of us,
spiritually speaking, is just like that skinny guy in the photo.
But once we let Jesus take over and He starts working in
us, everyone who sees us will say, "Wow! What a change!"

---

*Thank You, Jesus, for making me strong.
I know this kind of change would've
been impossible for me on my own.*

A STRONG HAND

Yet I am always with You. You hold me by my right hand.
You will lead me by telling me what I should do. And
after this, You will bring me into shining-greatness.
PSALM 73:23–24

When you were younger, did you get scared when you went to a new place? Lots of kids are relieved when their parent or grandparent holds their hand and says, "It's all right—just follow me." Suddenly, the fear fades away. If someone who loves you—someone you really trust—is making all the big decisions, life is much easier. It's not as scary.

Isn't it great that God holds our hand? As great and loving as a mom or dad or grandma or grandpa can be, the Creator of the universe is *so* much better. Even adults make mistakes sometimes, but God has never made a mistake—and never will.

So be strong and hold tightly to God's hand.

Take my hand, Lord, when I'm scared of what
might happen next. As long as You're guiding
me, I don't have to worry about anything.

ALL GOD WANTS

Let us give thanks all the time to God through
Jesus Christ. Our gift to Him is to give thanks.
Our lips should always give thanks to His name.
HEBREWS 13:15

How would you repay a mysterious stranger who saved
your life?

That's a tough question. Maybe you'd search your
house, looking for something valuable to give. Maybe
you'd promise to mow that person's yard for the next ten
years. Or maybe you'd plan to hand over a third of your
money to that person for the rest of your life.

Well, God has done more for you than a trillion of
these mysterious strangers combined. He's not only saved
your life—He's saved your *soul*. So what does He expect
in return?

Just your thanks.

God knows we can't possibly repay Him for His incredible gift—in fact, He'd be offended if we tried.
Instead, the only return payment He wants is our thankfulness. Why? Because thankfulness comes from the
heart, and our heart is all He's ever truly wanted.

Thank You, God, for doing everything for me. Help me
never to lose my sense of gratitude for Your gifts.

BAD NEWS

He will not be afraid of bad news. His heart
is strong because he trusts in the Lord.
PSALM 112:7

Hank came home from school one day worried sick.

There'd been a big test in math class that day, and Hank didn't know what kind of score he'd gotten. A lot of the questions had been really tough, and even though he *thought* he'd done well, what if he really hadn't?

That's when Hank remembered today's verse. He reminded himself that a strong boy "will not be afraid of bad news. His heart is strong because he trusts in the Lord."

Hank knew he'd studied well the night before, and he'd prayed right before he picked up his pencil. So what was the worst that could happen? Even if he got some "bad" news, he knew that God always has a reason for everything. No matter what, Hank trusted God to work it all out.

That night, Hank had no trouble falling asleep.

Help me, Lord, not to worry about bad news.
Even if something bad happens, I know
You'll turn it into something good.

BETTER THAN YOU KNOW YOURSELF

*O Lord, You have looked through me and have
known me. You know when I sit down and when
I get up. You understand my thoughts from far
away. You look over my path and my lying down.
You know all my ways very well. Even before
I speak a word, O Lord, You know it all.*
PSALM 139:1–4

Think about the words you said yesterday. Can you re-member them all? If so, you're either some kind of genius or you don't talk very much.

Imagine how smart God is in comparison. He knew every word you said yesterday before you even said them. Not only that, He knows all the words you'll say tomorrow, next week, next year, and for the rest of your life. He truly does know *everything*.

Because God knows all about us, we can be strong whenever the future looks dark and scary. After all, the same one who knows us also loves us—and He's always making sure to take care of His kids.

---

*Thank You, God, for knowing so much about
me—much more than I know about myself.*

THINGS THAT GO BUMP IN THE NIGHT

The Lord is my light and the One Who saves me.
Whom should I fear? The Lord is the strength
of my life. Of whom should I be afraid?
PSALM 27:1

When you were younger, how scared were you of the dark? When you woke up in the middle of the night, were your eyes drawn to that creepy shadow in the corner? Sure, you *knew* it was nothing more than a pile of clothes but try telling that to your racing heart. And what about that thing in the closet? *Is that arm reaching toward me?*

But when you jumped up and hit the light switch, all your fears vanished. The pile of clothes was just as harmless as ever, and that jacket sleeve in the closet couldn't hurt anyone. Relieved, you fell back asleep.

Thankfully, God is our light switch when life gets scary. So whenever worries keep you up at night, send up a prayer and watch as God drives away your fear.

Thank You, Lord, for allowing me to be strong,
even in the darkest night. I could never
be fearless without Your light.

GOD'S SELF-PORTRAIT

Then God said, "Let Us make man like Us and let him be head over the fish of the sea, and over the birds of the air, and over the cattle, and over all the earth, and over every thing that moves on the ground." And God made man in His own likeness. . . . He made both male and female.
GENESIS 1:26–27

A lot of famous artists create "self-portraits"—paintings of themselves. These paintings often sell for tons of money. Why? Because of the value of the artist who painted them.

Now imagine how much more valuable *God's* creation is. He's the biggest, most important Being in the universe, so anything He makes is priceless, let alone something that's made in His own "likeness."

That's exactly what humans are. And because we're made to look like God—maybe not physically, but spiritually—one soul is more valuable than the entire universe.

So the next time you feel down and unimportant, remember: you are God's self-portrait.

Thank You, Lord, for reminding me how much I'm truly worth. Help me to remember that fact— and to treat everyone else the same way too.

FIGHT

We break down every thought and proud thing that puts itself up against the wisdom of God. We take hold of every thought and make it obey Christ.
2 CORINTHIANS 10:5

"Break down" and "take hold." What do those phrases make you think of? Big battles against the enemy? An advancing army?

Today's verse isn't talking about warfare between tanks and planes. Rather, it's talking about the struggles that go on in your head.

You see, the devil's favorite weapon is something we usually overlook: our thoughts. *What if God isn't listening? What if God doesn't love me? What if God isn't even real?* Slowly, even a strong Christian boy might start letting these thoughts sink in—with terrible consequences.

Don't let the devil win a cheap victory over your brain. Fight back with God's Word and the peace that comes from being His kid. That's the only way you can "break down" the enemy's schemes.

Thank You, God, for giving me all the weapons I need to fight the devil.

HAPPY THOUGHTS

You will keep the man in perfect peace whose mind is kept on You, because he trusts in You.
ISAIAH 26:3

Have you ever heard a grown-up talking about "getting away from it all"? They think about beautiful beaches, fancy restaurants, and other things that make them happy. There's nothing wrong with that, of course. But we should never forget the one thing that always brings peace: God's love.

God's love isn't just an idea that we talk about; it's a real thing, just like a beach or restaurant, but far better. God's love is the reason we're alive, and it's the only thing that promises us a forever home with Him.

Take a few minutes each day to think about God's love—that should solve most of your worries in a hurry. During these moments of peace, God will grow your strength so that you'll be better able to face any bigger worries that come later.

So what are you waiting for? Think about God today.

Help me think about You, God, whenever I get worried. You're the only Person who can take away all my fears and replace them with Your peace.

WALK BY FAITH

"Do not worry about tomorrow. Tomorrow will have its own worries. The troubles we have in a day are enough for one day."
MATTHEW 6:34

Why doesn't God just tell us what will happen in the future?

This is a common question among Christians. After all, we know that God knows everything. So we wonder why He leaves us to stress over tomorrow.

There are two reasons why it's not a good idea for God to tell us everything. First, maybe we wouldn't *want* to know some things about the future. Sometimes God's plans involve a short time of pain before we get to His long-term benefits. Knowing that you're going to break your leg tomorrow would probably cause even more worry.

Second, if God told us the end of our stories, we'd feel no need to depend on Him. Life would be boring and predictable. We'd never have the reason to rise above our stress and walk by faith—which is exactly how God grows our strength.

Help me to walk by faith, Lord. I don't need to know what lies ahead. I know You have everything under control.

HEAVENLY BODYGUARDS

*For He will tell His angels to care for you and keep
you in all your ways. They will hold you up in their
hands. So your foot will not hit against a stone.*
PSALM 91:11–12

Famous and important people have bodyguards. Presidents, movie stars, and athletes have a lot of admirers, but sometimes they also have enemies. So they need people to protect them.

Well, God thinks each of His kids is unimaginably special, so He gives us bodyguards too: angels!

Today's verse doesn't teach that angels won't let you stub your toe. That's just a figure of speech. What it really means is that they will protect you in your walk with God. Nothing will happen to you that hasn't already been approved by Him. With God, there are no surprises.

So whenever the ground gets bumpy and you start to lose your footing, remember to call out to God. He and His angels will never let you fall.

---

*Thank You, Father, for making sure I'm
always protected. Knowing all these angels
are around me, I feel safe and strong.*

FEELING LIKE SUPERMAN

With Your help I can go against many soldiers.
With my God I can jump over a wall.
PSALM 18:29

You've heard of Superman, right? The first Superman comic book goes way back to 1938. He was famous for being "faster than a speeding bullet! More powerful than a locomotive! Able to leap tall buildings at a single bound!"

But heroes like Superman don't exist. . .do they?

Today's scripture says God gives each of His kids superhuman strength. No, we might not be able to lift up cars and punch out supervillains. But with God's help, we can lift life's heavy burdens and fend off Satan's attacks.

No matter what scary situations we find ourselves in, we don't have to cave under the pressure. Worry, fear, and weakness are useless words for a child of God. Instead, God wants us to stand tall, look the threat straight in the eye, and shout, "No need to fear—God is here."

Isn't that super?

Thank You, Jesus, for giving me power that I could never have on my own. Because of You, I'm not afraid of anything life can throw at me.

WHITE DOT

*Do not act like the sinful people of
the world. Let God change your life.*
ROMANS 12:2

Sometimes a speaker will hold up a white piece of paper
with a single black dot in the middle and ask, "What do
you see?" Naturally, people answer, "A black dot." Then
the speaker points out that they missed everything else on
the page—all the white.

This illustration can be used to prove how easy it is
for us to notice bad things, even when everything else is
good. But what if we flipped it around? What if the page
were black with a single *white* dot in the middle?

Today's verse calls for us to be that white dot.

You probably know a lot of people who aren't Christians. Maybe it seems everyone around you is doing
wrong. But if that's true, think how you can stand out if
you stay strong and do what's right.

When you let God change your life, you won't act like
the sinful people of the world. Some of them might even
want to know what makes you different.

---

*Lord, give me the bravery to stand up
for You, even if nobody else does.*

DON'T QUIT!

This is the reason we do not give up.
Our human body is wearing out. But our
spirits are getting stronger every day.
2 CORINTHIANS 4:16

Nolan had trained months for this race—much harder than any other student that he knew. But now, with the finish line in sight, the only thing on his mind was quitting.

His legs ached, his lungs burned, his heart hammered, and every inch of his body seemed to be screaming in pain. He could hear the second-place runner right behind him, and he knew that the moment he slowed down, his race would be over.

Even though his entire body wanted to quit, Nolan's determination won the day. He crossed the finish line, surrounded by cheering friends and family. Sure, it had been hard getting there—but he wouldn't trade his victory for anything.

When life gets you down and you feel like serving God is just not worth it any more, remember Nolan's example. Remind yourself of three things: the God you're running for, how far you've come, and what lies just beyond the finish line.

Then keep running.

Give me strength, Lord, to keep running for You.

CHOOSE, CHOSEN, OR BOTH?

*We know that God makes all things work
together for the good of those who love Him
and are chosen to be a part of His plan.*
ROMANS 8:28

Today's verse says people whom God has chosen have no need to fear—everything will work out in the end.

But wait, you might think, *How do I know if God has chosen me?* Easy: Romans 8:29 says, "God knew from the beginning who would put their trust in Him. So He chose them."

In other words, if you've decided to trust in God, then today's verse applies to you. You see, God knows everything, even things that haven't happened yet. This means God knew all your choices from the very beginning of the universe, including your decision on whether you wanted to be a part of His plan. And for everyone who would one day choose Him, He chose to work powerfully in their lives. Isn't that cool?

The only question that's left is this: What's your choice?

Lord, I choose You. Thank You for choosing me.

HE'S GOT YOU COVERED

*It is God Who covers me with strength
and makes my way perfect.*
PSALM 18:32

Have you ever seen a commercial for car insurance? Maybe you focused more on their funny jokes than what the ads were actually saying. Either way, you probably heard them say something like, "We've got you covered."

What that means is that if something bad happens to your car, the company will step in and pay for the damage. Because you've paid into their company, they'll "cover" the cost of your repairs.

Well, God has an insurance plan too, but it doesn't have anything to do with money. He promises to "cover" us with strength. When bad things happen and we don't have much courage, He'll give us some of His own. After all, He has plenty to spare.

The moment you trusted in Jesus, you signed up for this great plan. Not only does it offer a reason to never worry, but it also promises a life with God forever after this life is over.

As long as you're trusting in God, He's got you covered.

---

*Lord, I know that Your strength is enough for me to
face anything. Thank You for offering it to me.*

THE STRONGEST SONG OF ALL

"See, God saves me. I will trust and not be afraid.
For the Lord God is my strength and song.
And He has become the One Who saves me."
ISAIAH 12:2

Do you like music? Do certain songs—the words they use and the way they're sung—really make you feel the emotions the singer is feeling? Whenever you feel a certain way, do you listen to songs that match your emotions?

If so, today's verse will be especially meaningful. When the speaker says that God is his "song," he means that God is not just something worth singing about. God is the only reason he has for singing!

Strong boys realize that there's no song in the world better than the song God gives them. When you're feeling low and want to put on a sad song, remind yourself that God's music is upbeat. He's your strength and song, because He saves you.

Lord, You are my song. Help me sing
to You with everything I do and say.

TUNED IN

*Jesus said to her, "Martha, Martha, you are
worried and troubled about many things.
Only a few things are important, even just one."*
LUKE 10:41–42

It may be hard to believe, but your parents and grand-parents didn't always have perfect audio signals to listen to. They had to tune in to radio stations for music, and often there was static and other noise. Sometimes two radio stations were on the same frequency, interfering with each other. People might find a song they liked, but all the distractions made it impossible to enjoy it.

That's the idea of today's scripture. Martha had great intentions. She loved Jesus and wanted to hear His words, but she became so distracted by tiny, unimportant details that she started missing His teaching. She thought it was more important to cook dinner, for example, than to eat Jesus' bread of life. So He told her to tune out the noise, especially when it got in the way of what really mattered.

Are you "tuned in" to God's signal?

---

*Jesus, I know that the only way I can become
strong is by focusing on the one thing that
gives me strength—Your voice. Teach me
how to tune out the world's distractions.*

HAPPY, HAPPY, HAPPY

Be happy in the Lord. And He will
give you the desires of your heart.
PSALM 37:4

Doctors and experts on the brain agree that if you're feeling sad, it's easy to start doing things that make you even sadder. It's like a self-feeding sad machine—not a good thing at all.

But did you know God offers a different kind of self-feeding machine, one for happiness? Today's verse says that seeking happiness in the Lord will result in Him giving you "the desires of your heart," making you even happier.

This doesn't mean He'll always give you the newest gaming system. Instead, it means your heart will want the blessings He plans to give you. When you choose to be happy in God, He will make sure your happiness keeps growing and growing.

God loves growing the joy of Christian boys, especially those who look for the bright side in every situation. Where are *you* looking for happiness?

Help me, Lord, to seek happiness in You alone.

LOOK TO JESUS

*Let us keep looking to Jesus. Our faith comes
from Him and He is the One Who makes it perfect.
He did not give up when He had to suffer shame and
die on a cross. He knew of the joy that would be His
later. Now He is sitting at the right side of God.*
HEBREWS 12:2

"Keep looking to Jesus." What does that mean?

How does looking at Jesus' suffering help us to manage our own? Simple: because we know Jesus made it all the way through His pain, and now He's rooting us on.

When your friends make fun of you for your faith, look to Jesus. When you don't know if you can pass an important test and you're tempted to cheat, look to Jesus. When you really don't want to apologize to your friend, but you know it's the right thing to do, look to Jesus.

Whenever you look to Jesus on the cross, He'll give you the faith you need to make the right choice. So look to Him—and keep looking.

---

*Thank You, Jesus, for setting an example
I can look to when life gets hard.
Help me to never stop looking to You.*

HELPING HAND

*"For I am the Lord your God Who holds
your right hand, and Who says to you,
'Do not be afraid. I will help you.'"*
ISAIAH 41:13

The Bible says a lot about our being helped by God. But have you ever wondered how that actually works? Sometimes, God just performs miracles, getting us out of sticky situations right away. The Bible is full of such examples. But at other times, God is less dramatic.

John 14:26 says that the Holy Spirit is "the Helper" who will "teach you everything and help you remember everything I have told you." How this works is a mystery, but the important thing is that it *does*.

Also, God uses the Holy Spirit to give us the courage to do what's right. Peter, for example, really loved Jesus—but then he got afraid of other people and said he didn't even *know* Jesus. Once the Holy Spirit came down, Peter preached boldly to thousands of people.

No matter what you're facing, you can be strong, knowing that God is holding your hand.

---

*Lord, even when I can't see a way out,
I know You're going to lead me through.*

GOD KEEPS HIS PROMISES

*The angel said to the women, "Do not be afraid.
I know you are looking for Jesus Who was nailed
to the cross. He is not here! He has risen
from the dead as He said He would."*
MATTHEW 28:5–6

It's no secret that God always keeps His promises. But if those promises take a while, do we start to doubt God?

In Matthew 17:23, Jesus had predicted that He would die and then come out of the grave three days later. But now that He *was* dead and the sun was coming up on the third day, this amazing promise was probably the last thing on the disciples' minds.

Until it came true.

Sometimes, we get so distracted by how bad everything around us looks that we forget God's promise of eternal life with Him. But just as Jesus followed through and rose from the grave, He'll follow through and raise us up too.

Do you believe that?

---

*Thank You, Jesus, for all the comforting promises
You've made to me. Help me keep them in my mind
and remember them when I need them the most.*

GOD SINGS

*"The Lord your God is with you, a Powerful
One Who wins the battle. He will have much joy
over you. With His love He will give you new life.
He will have joy over you with loud singing."*
ZEPHANIAH 3:17

You've sung praise to God at church, haven't you? But did you know that God also sings over *you*? How is that possible?

The Bible tells us many times that God not only loves His followers but takes great delight in them (see Psalm 18:19; Psalm 147:11; Proverbs 12:22; and Romans 2:29). We're not just some pet in an outdoor cage—we're His very own kids. Isn't that something?

The next time you're feeling hopeless and sad, try singing a song of praise to God. And if you listen closely for His reply, you might just hear His own song echo back.

---

*Thank You, Lord, for letting me know that
You take joy in me. Help me to live my life
in a way that makes You even happier.*

HARD FAITH

Even if the fig tree does not grow figs and there is no fruit on the vines, even if the olives do not grow and the fields give no food, even if there are no sheep within the fence and no cattle in the cattle-building, yet I will have joy in the Lord. I will be glad in the God Who saves me.
HABAKKUK 3:17–18

Today's scripture is pretty tough, no matter how you look at it. Sure, it may be easy to say the words. But it's tougher to really *mean* what you say.

Imagine if everything you own—your games, bed, sofas, chairs, even your house—were just taken away. What would your first thought be? If you're like most people, you'd probably be upset, maybe even angry at God.

But Habakkuk knew none of that stuff really mattered—the only thing worth keeping was his relationship with God. And because nothing could take that away, he decided that nothing could take away his devotion to God.

Lord, give me strength so that, if everything I have is taken away, I can learn to trust in You even more.

BIG WORRIES, BIGGER PEACE

*Let the peace of Christ have power over
your hearts. You were chosen as a part
of His body. Always be thankful.*
COLOSSIANS 3:15

Aaron decided that Kevin was a mystery. Kevin's mom was
really sick, bullies picked on him, and he was getting ready
to move out of the state. And yet somehow, he was calm.

One day, Aaron decided to ask him about it. "Why
aren't you worried?" Aaron said. "If I were you, I'd be
a mess."

Kevin replied, "I *am* worried, Aaron. I feel awful every
time I think about it. But the reason I'm able to stay calm
is because Jesus' love is greater than my fear. No matter
what happens next, God will be there for me. Thinking
about *that* gives me enough peace to be strong."

Like Kevin, we'll all have hard times in our lives. But
thanks to God's love, our peace can be bigger than our
worry.

*God, I want Your peace to win against my worries.
Show me how to trust completely in You.*

GIVE IT ALL

Give all your worries to Him
because He cares for you.
1 Peter 5:7

The Bible talks a lot about giving to God. He wants us to give Him our time, our thanks, and even our whole lives. Giving is a great way of showing God just how seriously we take our relationship with Him.

But did you realize it's important to give God your worries? *Why would God want my worries?* you may ask. *I don't even want them myself.*

That's the point. God knows that worries only drag you down. They get in the way of your relationship with Him. If you hang on to worries, you're only hurting yourself. And God doesn't want that to happen.

Once you hand over every part of your life to God—even the parts you don't want Him to know about—He can replace them with a brand-new life. And He'll start growing you into the boy He's always intended for you to be.

Thank You, Father, for promising to
take care of my load. I don't want
to hold anything back from You.

JOY METER

*"Until now you have not asked for anything
in My name. Ask and you will receive.
Then your joy will be full."*
JOHN 16:24

Have you ever gotten an amazing Christmas present? Maybe it was a new bicycle, a video game, or an expensive gadget you'd asked for months earlier. At that moment, how high was your "joy meter"?

Today's verse says that when we ask God for something in Jesus' name, He'll give it to us. And when He does, our joy meter will be all the way to the top.

Of course, this doesn't mean you can just ask Him for anything—He probably won't give you a million dollars just because you asked, for instance. Rather, it means that when you ask for something that He *wants* you to ask for—in His name—then He'll be more than happy to watch your eyes light up with joy when He gives it to you.

What are you asking God for today?

---

*Thank You, Jesus, for promising to give me so much joy.
Help me ask for things that You'll be happy to give.*

ON YOUR MIND

Never stop praying.
1 THESSALONIANS 5:17

Some Christian monks take today's verse very seriously, scheduling many hours each day for prayer. In fact, throughout the day, they do little else. Some ancient monks took this even further and prayed—quite literally—*all day long.*

These monks, of course, aren't doing anything wrong. In fact, it's great that they're so devoted to God. But what about the rest of us? For most people, many hours of prayer and meditation just aren't possible.

But thankfully, today's verse isn't talking about that. Paul, the writer of 1 Thessalonians, was busy most of the time too—making tents, preaching the gospel, and building churches. When he wrote today's verse, he meant for us to never *forget* about prayer.

When things happen, good or bad, we should always make it a habit of tossing up quick prayers to God. And by keeping prayer on our minds throughout the day, we'll remember the one to whom we're praying. And that's a great way to make us stronger.

I never want to forget to pray, Lord. Teach me how to keep You on my mind, no matter where I am or what I'm doing.

"KNOWING" AND "UNDERSTANDING"

I pray that. . .He will make you strong with power in your hearts through the Holy Spirit. I pray that Christ may live in your hearts by faith. I pray that you will be filled with love. I pray that you will be able to understand how wide and how long and how high and how deep His love is. I pray that you will know the love of Christ.
EPHESIANS 3:16–19

God's love isn't something you can understand just by studying it. We can "know" that it's so deep that it never ends, but there's no way we can "understand" that until we experience it for ourselves. And once we do, we don't walk away as the same person—we're made "strong with power" as His love rushes through our veins.

Thankfully, if you're a child of God, that's exactly what He's doing in your life right now. You may not feel it right away, but over time, you'll start to see just how deep His love really runs and how deeply He's changing you into the strong boy you're meant to be.

How awesome is *that*?

---

*Help me understand Your love, Jesus.
I want to be made strong in You.*

BIG QUESTIONS

*"The secret things belong to the Lord our God.
But the things that are made known belong
to us and to our children forever, so we
may obey all the words of this Law."*
DEUTERONOMY 29:29

Many people complain about things they don't under-stand. "If God really loves everyone," they say, "why would He let this happen?" And there are plenty of other mys-teries that keep people up at night—mysteries that we'll probably never be able to answer.

But today's verse teaches that that's okay. We don't need to know everything. If we knew half of God's biggest secrets, after all, our heads would probably explode.

Instead, God decided to reveal to us everything we need to know about Him through the Bible. His love, justice, and reward for His kids—all that and more is found in its pages. But once our life here is over, we won't need the Bible anymore: we'll see God face to face. There'll be no need for wondering or guessing. We'll have forever to ask Him any question we'd like.

---

*Lord, help me be strong enough to
accept what I can't yet understand.*

WATCHING EYE

I will show you and teach you in the
way you should go. I will tell you
what to do with My eye upon you.
PSALM 32:8

"I've got my eye on you."

How often have you heard someone use this expression? Most likely, that person's tone of voice wasn't very positive. The words seemed to mean, "If you mess up again, then watch out!"

Today's verse says that God has His "eye upon you." But unlike the people who usually say this, He's not being critical or threatening. Instead, He's speaking much like a teacher who helps a struggling student with a hard project. He steps back and lets us try our best, and whenever we mess up or need help, He steps back in and tells us what to do next. That way, He strengthens us, improving our words and actions while also causing us to trust more in Him.

Today, thank God for the fact that He's got His eye on you.

Thank You, God, for not leaving me by myself to fail.
Help me to never be afraid of Your watching eye.

CRUEL WHISPERS

"Do not say what is wrong in other people's lives. Then other people will not say what is wrong in your life. Do not say someone is guilty. Then other people will not say you are guilty. Forgive other people and other people will forgive you."
LUKE 6:37

Lucas loved talking with his friends each day at lunch. But lately, he noticed something strange: it seemed all their conversations were about other people. And they weren't exactly nice conversations, either.

At first, Lucas went along with it, even throwing in a few jabs of his own. But one day, as he walked by the table, he heard his *own* name whispered, followed by a bunch of mean laughter. But as anger rose up in his heart, he remembered all the times he'd done the same thing to others. He didn't realize how much it hurt until it happened to him.

Jesus, whenever I'm tempted to talk about someone, help me to consider how I'd feel if those words were said about me. Then cause me to replace that insult with a compliment.

STAYING WARM

I will have much joy in the Lord. My soul will have joy in my God, for He has clothed me with the clothes of His saving power. He has put around me a coat of what is right and good.
ISAIAH 61:10

Whenever you go out in the snow, what's the first thing you do? Unless you love feeling your skin go numb and your teeth clatter against each other, you probably bundle up. With a coat and gloves on, it's harder for the cold to get to you.

Today's world is filled with people who do wrong things. And if you're not careful, all that wrong can seep under your skin and straight to your heart. That's why God promises to give us a "coat of what is right and good." As long as we're wearing the clothing He provides—by reading our Bible and being led by His Spirit—we can be protected from the chilly world around us.

It's cold out there today. Are you dressed for winter?

Clothe me with strength and a sense of right and wrong, God. Help my life to be a warm spot in a cold world.

PERILOUS PATHS

*Your Word is a lamp to my feet
and a light to my path.*
PSALM 119:105

The brave explorer walked slowly through the cave, surrounded by the sounds of dripping water and the chirping of tiny bats. Everything was dark except for the torch he held in front of him. The flickering light shone on the path ahead, revealing spiders and foul-smelling water on both sides. But he kept walking, confident that the torch would guide him to safety.

God's Word is like that torch. Our entire life is one big adventure, and there are times when we might not know if we're going to make it out okay. But while God doesn't usually tell us how our problems will end, He does gives us just enough information to press on. Step by step, we can trust in His Word for each small decision we make.

Like that brave explorer, we'll find that the treasure awaiting us will be worth every second of danger we face.

---

*Thank You, God, for giving me the Bible
as a light. Help me to use it wisely.*

LEAP OF FAITH

You have never seen Him but you love Him. You cannot see Him now but you are putting your trust in Him. . . . You will get what your faith is looking for, which is to be saved from the punishment of sin.
1 PETER 1:8–9

Putting our faith in God is a big deal—so big, in fact, that it affects every part of our lives. It's like stepping off a cliff, trusting that someone whom you've never seen will catch you on the way down.

But fortunately, God doesn't just say "trust Me" without any reason. He's given us all kinds of reasons to know He's in the beautiful world around us, in every blessing of our lives, and in the promises of His Word. Trusting God isn't a leap in the dark—it's the most reasonable thing to do.

Sure, it can be scary to have have faith, but God's already taken care of everything. All you have to do is jump.

Thank You, God, for helping me along as I try to trust in You. I want my faith to grow stronger each day.

MUDDIED WATERS

Live and work without pride. Be gentle and kind.
Do not be hard on others. . . . Work hard to live together as
one by the help of the Holy Spirit. Then there will be peace.
EPHESIANS 4:2–3

Pride is like a blob of mud. If you drop that into a sparkling, crystal-clear glass of water, everything changes. The water suddenly becomes disgusting. You don't want to drink it.

A healthy relationship between two friends is one of the most beautiful things in the world. But the moment a little pride seeps in, it doesn't take long for that relationship to turn ugly and cruel. Kind words change to insults. Love turns to jealousy. Good memories turn into regrets.

It takes a strong boy to let God wash the pride out of his heart. Admitting the pride is there is the first (and hardest) step toward allowing Him to deal with it. But once you take that step, God will be sure to follow through.

Lord, I don't want pride to spoil my relationships
with my friends, my family, and You. I want
to be at peace with everyone.

DON'T BE A LEMMING

*"When the shepherd walks ahead of them,
they follow him because they know his voice."*
JOHN 10:4

You may have heard about how lemmings dive off the edge of a cliff simply because "everyone else is doing it."

Well, that isn't quite accurate. It *is* true, however, that lemmings—a kind of small rodent—will sometimes try swimming across a river that's just too wide. From this dangerous game of "follow the leader," many drown.

Sheep are similar—they're always looking for a leader to follow. But there's one difference: sheep have shepherds to guide them, lemmings do not.

Today's verse calls you to be a sheep, not a lemming. God doesn't want any of us to follow the crowd. That leads to disappointment and hopelessness. Instead, God says we should follow His Son, Jesus, our shepherd. Not only will He never lead us off a cliff, but He'll lead us into the greenest pastures we've ever seen.

So who are you following today?

---

*Thank You, God, for promising to lead me
to safety. Help me to be strong and
wise enough to follow Your voice.*

WORRIED SICK

*"Which of you can make yourself a little taller
by worrying? If you cannot do that which is
so little, why do you worry about other things?"*
LUKE 12:25–26

Logan hated the thought of getting sick. He'd had the flu before, and he did *not* want to go through that again.

But instead of just washing his hands and trusting God, Logan chose to worry. A lot. Whenever his friends were out playing, Logan sat inside, looking anxiously out the window and hoping a germ didn't float in.

Soon, the unthinkable happened: Logan began feeling ill.

How'd this happen? he fussed. When he went to the doctor and told him what was wrong, the doctor just smiled.

"Relax, Logan," the doctor said. "There's nothing wrong with you, other than the fact that you've worried too much. Did you know worrying can make you sick?"

Jesus' words in today's scripture show us just how foolish worrying can be. Not only is it completely useless, but it can be harmful as well. Thankfully, with God by our side, there's no need to worry ourselves sick.

Help me replace my worry with trust, God.

NOT STRONG ENOUGH

*And so Jesus is able, now and forever, to save from
the punishment of sin all who come to God through
Him because He lives forever to pray for them.*
HEBREWS 7:25

How strong do you think you are? Maybe you're really
good in gym class and can lift a lot of weight compared
to other boys your age. Maybe you imagine yourself as
winning tough-guy competitions someday.

But no matter how strong you get, there will always
be one thing you can't do: save yourself from sin.

God is perfect, so for Him to accept anyone into a life
with Him, that person has to be perfect too. The problem
is, nobody on earth is perfect! We've all sinned in one way
or another, and we all deserve to be punished.

That's why Jesus died on the cross—He took the
punishment that we deserve. Only He was strong enough
to pull heaven down to earth and provide the forgiveness
we need.

So if you're looking for strength, look no further than
Jesus.

---

*Thank You, Jesus, for being strong
enough to fill in for my weakness.*

WHERE TO LOOK

*"Look to the Lord and ask for
His strength. Look to Him all the time."*
1 CHRONICLES 16:11

Looking to the Lord can be hard, especially when other voices compete for our attention. When right and wrong seem blurry and we're not sure which decision to make, it's tempting to look to ourselves first. "If it feels good, do it," some people say. "Follow your heart."

The problem with that is that our hearts are not very reliable. "Go on, cheat on that test," your heart may say. "It's all right to be dishonest once in a while. You *deserve* it."

In cases like that, your heart might make some pretty convincing arguments. But a quick look at God's Word will show that your heart is talking nonsense. The more you dive into the Bible, the more strength you'll have to resist those sweet-sounding voices.

---

*Lord, I don't want to listen to false voices—even
the ones that come from my own heart. Help
me stay in Your Word so that whenever I need
to look for You, I won't have to look far.*

ROTTEN FRUIT

But the fruit that comes from having the Holy
Spirit in our lives is: love, joy, peace, not giving up,
being kind, being good, having faith, being gentle,
and being the boss over our own desires.
GALATIANS 5:22–23

Imagine going to the grocery store for some fruit, only to find that the entire produce aisle is full of rotten food. The bananas are all black and slimy, the apples have mold all over them, and the grapes look more like gross raisins.

You'd probably never shop there again, would you?

You're kind of like that store. God wants you to be full of the Holy Spirit's fruit. But if you stop letting Him work and instead try to do your own thing, it won't be long before your fruit starts shriveling. Pretty soon, all that's left is nasty stuff—fake smiles and bitter attitudes. People will notice—both Christian friends and the nonbelievers you've been trying to reach.

Nobody wants to shop at that store! Spend time in God's Word, stay connected to Jesus, and let the Holy Spirit grow His sweet, nourishing fruit in you.

I want You to grow my spiritual fruit, God.
Help me to allow You to work in my life.

BABY'S FIRST STEPS

*The steps of a good man are led by the Lord.
And He is happy in his way. When he falls, he will
not be thrown down, because the Lord holds his hand.*
PSALM 37:23–24

When a toddler is learning to walk, he doesn't learn by himself. His parents are always by his side, holding his hand and cheering him on. Sometimes, he'll trip over a table leg or a bump in the carpet, but that's okay—his parents are right there, ready to lift him back up again. At that moment, nothing in the world is more important to them than their child's success.

God, our heavenly Father, shows the same amount of concern toward His kids. When you fall—and don't fool yourself, you will—He's not up there laughing or criticizing you. Instead, He's right by your side, picking you up and setting you back on your feet.

With God as your loving parent, you'll eventually learn not only to walk but to run.

Thank You, God, for guiding my feet when my steps get wobbly. Help me to never resist Your helping hand.

BULLETPROOF

As for God, His way is perfect. The Word of the Lord has stood the test. He is a covering for all who go to Him for a safe place.
PSALM 18:30

Police officers put a lot of faith in their bulletproof vests. Whenever they face bad guys, this vest could be the difference between life or death. But how do they know if their vest will even work?

It's simple: the company that makes those vests tests their product before sending it along to the police. After many, many bullets have been fired at many, many vests, the company can finally say, "Okay, we know our vests are safe."

God's Word is like a bulletproof vest. Throughout history, many people have "fired bullets" at it trying to prove it wrong. But the Bible still stands strong. You can trust it with your life.

When it comes to God's Word, your spiritual safety is guaranteed. You're bulletproof.

Thank You, God, for providing such a powerful vest as Your Word. I know it can stop any weapons the devil tries to lob at me—so help me make good use of it today.

TROUBLED HEARTS

*"Do not let your heart be troubled. You have put
your trust in God, put your trust in Me also."*
JOHN 14:1

Imagine yourself in the disciples' shoes. You've followed
Jesus for three years, watched as He performed mind-
boggling miracles, and listened to His teaching about
the kingdom of God. You believe He's the promised Savior who will one day lead your people to freedom. Jesus
is your whole world. But now He says He's going to die?
How could your heart *not* be troubled by such news?

But Jesus also promised that He would rise again—
a promise they somehow quickly forgot.

Sometimes, Jesus steps back for a bit to let us use
what we've learned. During those times, we may feel
scared and uncertain, but we should always remember
His promise to return. He's done everything else He
said He would do. There's no reason to let your heart be
troubled.

---

*Lord, I know You never leave my side, even when
I can't feel You. Thank You for giving me reasons
to have peace in my heart each day.*

YOURS TO KEEP

*"You are sad now. I will see you again
and then your hearts will be full of joy.
No one can take your joy from you."*
JOHN 16:22

Think of the safest place on the planet. Is it a bank vault? The president's limousine? A secret underground military base?

Well, today's verse mentions a place that's more secure than any of these locations—your heart.

Once you give your heart to God, He stuffs it full of priceless treasures and puts a lock on it that nobody else can open. Inside are salvation, peace, hope and, of course, joy. All these things combine to make you stronger in Him.

Because God has made your heart so secure, the only way anyone could steal your treasure is if you handed it over to them. But if you stay close to Jesus and let Him work in your life, there's no chance anyone can reach it. The treasure is yours and yours to keep.

Thank You, Jesus, for giving me a treasure no one can steal. I never want to give it away.

JUST ASK

*"Ask, and what you are asking for will be
given to you. . . . Knock, and the door you
are knocking on will be opened to you."*
MATTHEW 7:7

In the famous book *The Lord of the Rings*, the main characters find a magical door with a message reading, "Speak, friend, and enter." Unsure of the password, Gandalf, the group's leader, rattles off a list of words and phrases, hoping that one of them will be correct.

But, eventually, he realizes that the instructions aren't complicated—all he needs to do is speak the word *friend*.

Sometimes people make it more confusing to come to God than they need to. But the Bible's way is simple: "Knock, and the door. . .will be opened." To get to God's forgiveness and strength, you don't need to know a special code—all you need to do is speak.

---

*Thank You, Lord, for allowing me to come to
You so easily. Help me to never complicate
what You've designed to be simple.*

LAUGHTER—THE BEST MEDICINE

A glad heart is good medicine,
but a broken spirit dries up the bones.
PROVERBS 17:22

The Bible is full of instructions on how to follow God and reach heaven. But it also has lots of simple advice that applies to everyday life, especially in the book of Proverbs.

One bit of advice is something you might even find at a doctor's office—happiness is good for you. Not only does it brighten your day, but it actually gives you strength.

It's true: whenever you're feeling down, your body gets sick a lot more easily. You start feeling weak, which then makes you feel even sadder. But if you break the cycle by forcing yourself to laugh (whether it's at a funny joke or even at something you did), you'll suddenly be on your way toward health once more.

Because God is so smart, He put this advice in today's verse as a way of allowing His kids to be healthier. He wants us to be strong—in every sense of the word.

Help me remember to laugh, God, even when I don't feel like it. I want to have a glad heart each day.

THE REAL THING

*God is the One Who makes our faith and your faith strong
in Christ. . . . He has put His mark on us to show we
belong to Him. His Spirit is in our hearts to prove this.*
2 CORINTHIANS 1:21–22

Have you ever seen something at the store that looked
almost identical to a more expensive item? If so, how did
you know which was which?

Chances are, you looked at the logo.

If something is the "good" brand, it'll have the company's signature in big, plain letters somewhere on the
box. Other companies can try all they want to imitate its
look, but they can't use the logo. It's against the law. The
logo, then, lets you know that you've got "the real thing."

Well, God places His logo—His Spirit—in us whenever we get saved. Without God's Spirit, none of us would
know if we're really part of His family. But because we
feel Him in our hearts, strengthening us with His love,
we know for sure that we have "the real thing."

---

*Thank You, God, for Your Spirit. Help me
never doubt if what I have is truly real.*

ONE DAY AT A TIME

*"No man will be able to stand against you all the days of
your life. I will be with you just as I have been with Moses.
I will be faithful to you and will not leave you alone."*

JOSHUA 1:5

For some kids, the thought of growing seems scary. Some
get nervous about taking on new responsibilities. Some
feel comfortable just where they are right now—and
never want to leave.

But change is a part of life. One day, you will be a
grown-up, working a job and paying bills and doing all the
things that grown-ups do. But for now, when you're still
a kid, it's just fine to enjoy your friends and family and
activities as they are. God wants you to enjoy the life you
have today without worrying about tomorrow.

But He also want you to know that whatever happens
in that place called "the future," He'll be right by your side,
just like He is right now.

---

*Thank You, God, for promising that I'll never be alone.
Help me to enjoy each moment as I rest in Your peace.*

THERE'S THE JOY

Be full of joy always because you belong to
the Lord. Again I say, be full of joy!
PHILIPPIANS 4:4

Today's verse tells us to "be full of joy." But how is that possible? Is joy just a switch that you turn on and off whenever you want?

Not quite. It's impossible to force yourself to feel joy. You can smile until your face hurts, but you'll probably end up no more joyful than when you began.

Instead, God says that your joy comes "because you belong to the Lord." If you're not one of God's kids, true joy is impossible. But if you are, all it takes is a reminder, and *bam!*—there's the joy. It doesn't come about by your own efforts; it happens because God has given it to you. The only question is whether you'll accept it.

Strong boys remember that no matter how tough life gets, being a child of the great Creator is more than enough reason to rejoice.

I'm joyful, Lord, because I belong to You. Thank You for brightening my life and giving me true happiness.

A GOOD START

*"See, I will do a new thing. It will begin happening
now. Will you not know about it? I will even make a
road in the wilderness, and rivers in the desert."*
ISAIAH 43:19

What do a road in the wilderness and a river in the desert
have in common? Both are a good start.

The road is a great way to bring life to a place that
would otherwise see nothing but sand and rocks. People
would begin traveling there, so the chances of a few
houses and towns cropping up would suddenly get higher.
And the river? It *literally* brings life. Any seeds that fall
on its banks will grow up into beautiful trees, attracting
birds and animals from all directions.

When God comes into your life, He starts putting
roads and rivers all through your soul. Your inside life,
which was once dull and without purpose, suddenly gets
bright and full of activity. Your spiritual strength, which
was once weak like a scraggly tree, starts to grow faster
than you ever thought possible.

Where a desert used to be, God plants a rainforest.

---

*Thank You, God, for taking my old life
and transforming it into something new.*

DANCING TO A NEW TUNE

*How happy are the people who know the sound
of joy! They walk in the light of Your face, O Lord.*
PSALM 89:15

Imagine you're at a friend's house, and his speakers are playing a song that you really hate. Ugh—you can't wait for the song to end. Everything about it annoys you.

Now imagine that when that crummy song finally ends, your all-time favorite song comes on. Your eyes brighten, you sit up straighter, you even start tapping your foot and singing along.

Today's scripture says that for people who know God, it's like their favorite song is always on—the song of joy. Just the thought of their old life annoys them, so they try to avoid it at all costs. Instead, they focus on the song that's playing right now, happy that it will never end.

Work on getting to know God better, every day and in every way. There's joy to be found there.

---

*Lord God, I never want to go back to the old,
rotten song of my life. May I walk in Your
light and know the sound of Your joy.*

CHANGING FAST

Jesus Christ is the same yesterday
and today and forever.
HEBREWS 13:8

Three years after Dylan had moved, his parents finally agreed to let him go back and visit one of his old friends.

When Dylan arrived in his hometown, things seemed off. Some buildings were gone, and lots of new people were walking on the street. When he finally met with his friend, Dylan was shocked to learn that many of his other acquaintances had moved. It seemed like nothing was the same.

Dylan was right—nothing does stay the same. Nothing except Jesus, that is.

Whenever everything around you is changing fast, you can take comfort in knowing that Jesus is the same now as He's been throughout all eternity. This means He's dependable: you can go to Him any time with any need, and He'll be sure to answer.

There's no greater way to grow strong than to get your strength from the one who never changes.

Thank You, Lord, for staying the same. Change can be scary, but I know I'll always have You to depend on.

WAIT FOR IT

It is good that one should be quiet and
wait for the saving power of the Lord.
LAMENTATIONS 3:26

Have you ever found yourself eagerly waiting for something? Maybe you were really hungry for dinner, but your mom said it would still be another thirty minutes. Or maybe it was something longer-term, like getting a test score back or going on a fun vacation.

If it's so hard to wait for things that we know all about, it's super tough to wait for God. After all, we can't even *see* Him. Much of the time, we don't have any idea of His specific plan. What we do know is that God knows best, and that His plan will come about in the perfect time and way.

Next time you're frustrated about waiting for something small, remember this: it might be a way that God is strengthening your patience for the things that really matter.

I know that waiting is a part of life, God, and that
it will boost my faith in You. So teach me to wait.

SOARING EAGLES

But they who wait upon the Lord will get new strength.
They will rise up with wings like eagles. They will run and
not get tired. They will walk and not become weak.
ISAIAH 40:31

Eagles are amazing creatures. Whenever a thunderstorm hits, they don't hunker down and hide like most other birds. Instead, they pull off one of the coolest stunts in all of nature—they use the wind of the storm to soar *above* the clouds. Below them, the lightning still flashes and the winds still roar, but the eagles don't care. The only thing they feel is the warm light of the sun above.

When you put your trust in God, He gives you eagle's wings. When life throws all its ugly tricks at you, that's just an opportunity to show more faith. And as you do, the peace you feel will be even greater than it was when everything was calm.

Next time you get worried, remember the eagle—and soar.

Give me wings like eagles, God. I want to use every
hard situation as a chance to grow closer to You.

CHAOS

*There is a special time for everything. There is a
time for everything that happens under heaven.*
ECCLESIASTES 3:1

Think how messed up everything would be if none of our
activities had a special time and place. You'd see people playing golf in the classroom, dancing and singing in
restaurants, playing video games while driving, and doing
jumping jacks at weddings.

Okay, so some of that might sound fun to you. But
think about it: if everyone did whatever he wanted whenever he wanted to, very little good would ever get done.
Even worse, some of these activities would certainly become very dangerous.

That's why today's verse says, "There is a special time
for everything." No matter how much we want a certain
thing to happen *right now*, God knows the perfect time
for it.

Strong boys understand that God isn't just trying to
frustrate us and make us wait for no reason. Instead, He's
working behind the scenes, making sure everything works
out for our good.

---

*Thank You, Jesus, for being so thoughtful about
what happens in my life and when. Without Your
wisdom, everything would be pointless.*

YOUR FIRST BITE

O taste and see that the Lord is good.
How happy is the man who trusts in Him!
PSALM 34:8

Can you remember the first time you ate your favorite food? Chances are, you weren't sure about it at first. *I'm not sure I'm going to like this,* you may have thought. But the moment you took your first bite, you realized you couldn't just stop there. You had to have more.

It's similar for many people when God promises to give joy, peace, and salvation. We may be a little hesitant at first. *What if it's not true?* we think. But once we try Him, we realize that our lives will never be the same. We have to have more.

And as long as we follow this desire that God gives us, we'll never want to go back to the way things were. Instead, we'll grow stronger and stronger as we eat up God's goodness.

Have you tasted and seen that the Lord is good yet?

Lord, I can't get enough of You.
I want You to keep feeding me with
Your truth and love for as long as I live.

117

THE GOD WHO SEES

*So Hagar gave this name to the Lord Who spoke
to her, "You are a God Who sees." For she said,
"Have I even stayed alive here after seeing Him?"*
GENESIS 16:13

Some people, when they think of God, imagine an old man in the sky, looking down from the clouds with a lightning bolt in his hand.

But our best imagination can't begin to describe who God really is. First, He is a spirit, meaning He doesn't have a body like us. Second, He's not floating on a cloud somewhere up high. (Come on, if that were true, He'd only be able to see one side of the earth at a time.) No, God is everywhere at once. And finally, He's not looking for reasons to hurt us for doing wrong. Instead, God patiently hopes for us to reconsider. He even nudges us in the right direction when we need it.

Today, give thanks to the God who not only sees but cares.

---

*Thank You, God, for seeing me where I am.
I know that I can be strong because
You surround me with Your love.*

BIG IMAGINATION

God is able to do much more than we ask
or think through His power working in us.
EPHESIANS 3:20

How big is your imagination? Do you struggle to come up with simple stories? Or are you the kind of guy who creates whole universes—filled with exciting characters—in your mind?

Whichever type you are, maybe you've wondered exactly what God has in store for your future. Maybe you've even made plans for your life that you think God should follow.

Well, today's verse promises that no matter how big your imagination is, you'll never be able to guess all the amazing things God will do in your life. The moment you think you have Him figured out, He'll surprise you with something you never thought of.

New things can be stressful. But new things are also exciting. God lets us all feel stress sometimes, but when we follow Him closely, it will definitely be exciting. Let your imagination run free—God is planning incredible things for your life.

I know Your imagination is much bigger than mine,
Lord. I want to give You control over my future.

UNSPLITTABLE

*We do not look at the things that can be seen. We
look at the things that cannot be seen. The things
that can be seen will come to an end. But the
things that cannot be seen will last forever.*
2 CORINTHIANS 4:18

You've probably heard that atoms are the "building blocks"
of everything that exists. But did you know that even atoms can be split apart? Yes, you can keep splitting matter until you get to a tiny particle called a "quark." (Funny
name, huh?)

It seems that quarks *can't* be split. They're the only
things in the universe that you can't break apart.

Our faith works the same way. Everything around us
has an end—the school year, our friendships, our homes,
and even our lives on earth. But the things we *can't* see—
God, His love, our souls, and heaven—are the things that
last forever.

That's why it's so important to put our trust in God.
Only He can give us a hope that can't be split apart.

---

*Grow my faith, God. Help me realize that the
most real things are the things I can't see.*

AWE AND WONDER

"All of you be quiet before the Lord.
For He is coming from His holy place."
ZECHARIAH 2:13

Imagine you're at a really important event, and the president of the United States is about to arrive. Everyone is chattering and laughing until suddenly, *he* walks in. Instantly, you and everyone else shape up as this important man walks to the stage. A strange electricity fills the air as the president clears his throat and prepares to talk.

Today's verse paints a similar picture. Only it's *God* who's walking in this time. He's more important than all the presidents and kings who've ever lived. And do you know where God is heading when He walks in? How about this: your heart.

When we're in the presence of God, it's only natural to feel a sense of deep respect. But we should also be excited and strengthened. After all, who doesn't want to be near the Creator of the universe?

Thank You, God, for being near to me each day. It's an honor that I don't deserve, but You stick around anyway. Help me never to lose my sense of awe and wonder.

A PLACE YOU'LL LOVE

*He lets me rest in fields of green grass. He leads
me beside the quiet waters. He makes me strong
again. He leads me in the way of living right with
Himself which brings honor to His name.*
PSALM 23:2–3

Bradly loved blackberries. One day, his friend Jeffery said,
"Hey! Come with me. I know a place you'll *love*."

Jeffery led Bradly down a little dirt path. A few minutes later, as they rounded a bend, Bradly's jaw nearly hit
the ground. Blackberry vines stretched out as far as the
eye could see.

Bradly came home that day with a bucket full of ber-
ries and a happy heart.

When we go looking for strength and peace, God
doesn't leave us to look alone. He takes our hand and
says, "Hey! Over here! I know a place where you'll *never*
have to be afraid again."

---

*Thank You, Jesus, for letting me know where
I can find everything I'll ever need. Lead me
until I reach my final home with You.*

HARD PUTTY

But now, O Lord, You are our Father.
We are the clay, and You are our pot maker.
All of us are the work of Your hand.
ISAIAH 64:8

Ever messed with Silly Putty or Play-Doh? If so, you know how fun it is to create people and animals and who-knows-what from your imagination.

But what happens if the putty hardens and refuses to bend? Your creative designs would be impossible. The putty would be pretty much useless.

Today's verse says you are like putty in God's hands. If you'll let Him, He'll change you into an amazing creation—a walking example of His goodness and power. But if you stiffen and refuse to budge, you'll live an unhappy life that doesn't accomplish anything.

Stay flexible. Don't allow yourself to get hard and stale. When you allow God to do whatever He wants in your life, you'll be happier, better, stronger.

Lord, I want to be like putty in Your hands.
Shape my soul into something that everyone else
can look at and say, "Look how amazing God is!"

PERFECT PROMISE KEEPER

"See, I am with you. I will care for you everywhere you go. And I will bring you again to this land. For I will not leave you until I have done all the things I promised you."

GENESIS 28:15

Have your parents or grandparents ever made you a big promise but then couldn't follow through because something happened?

Maybe they said they'd take you on a great vacation, but someone got sick and you all had to stay home. Maybe they promised a family game night, but instead they had to fix the refrigerator that stopped working. When your hopes are high and then you're disappointed, it's really tough to take.

God, however, is different. He makes promises all the time—and He's never broken a single one. He knows everything that will ever happen, so He can't be caught by surprise.

It takes strength to put your trust completely in God's promises, but it's worth it. And as you do, God will give you even more strength to believe.

Thank You, God, for being the perfect promise keeper. Remind me of Your trustworthiness whenever I doubt.

TREES BY THE RIVER

"Good will come to the man who trusts in the Lord, and whose hope is in the Lord. He will be like a tree planted by the water, that sends out its roots by the river. . . . It will not be troubled in a dry year, or stop giving fruit."
JEREMIAH 17:7–8

Have you ever noticed how often rivers and streams are lined by trees? There's a reason for that—the regular source of water is great for tree roots. When a seed takes hold on a river or creek bank, it puts out roots that spread far and deep and create a healthy tree.

This is a picture of the strong boy who trusts in God. His "living water" is a source of health and power, so when you plant yourself near Him—when you dig deep into His Word and spend quality time in prayer—you'll grow stronger and stronger.

Even through the storms and dry spells of life, you'll be okay if you've planted your roots deep in God. Make that your goal, today and every day.

God, grow my roots so that I can always find You.

TRAPPED

*I did not give up waiting for the Lord. And He turned
to me and heard my cry. He brought me up out of
the hole of danger, out of the mud and clay. He
set my feet on a rock, making my feet sure.*
PSALM 40:1–2

Kip was terrified. One second, he was hiking with his dad
on an autumn afternoon, pointing out the colorful leaves—
and the next, he was lying on his back in a ravine.

He tried to climb up, but Kip couldn't get a good
handhold. Then he saw his dad above, digging into his
backpack. He pulled out a coil of rope and let the end
down to Kip! Kip grabbed on and his dad started pulling
him up. Soon, Kip was looking down at where he'd been,
thanking his dad for his help.

Like Kip, we all occasionally find ourselves in a pit—a
pit of sin. We have to admit to God that we're stuck. But
once we do, He's eager to let down the rope of His love
and pull us out.

Thank You, Jesus, for lifting me up out of sin.

SMILE, PRINCE

But you are a chosen group of people. . . . You belong to God. He has done this for you so you can tell others how God has called you out of darkness into His great light.
1 PETER 2:9

Imagine being the adopted son of a powerful king. Before you were adopted, you lived under an old stone bridge. But then the king saw you and decided, *No, I want to give this boy so much more.* So he took you into his palace, where you met other sons and daughters—thousands of them—each one sharing a similar story.

But that's when the real shocker came in: your new dad promised that when you all grew up, you'd be kings and queens too, ruling right beside him on the throne.

That's what God did for you. He adopted you, erased your guilt, and promised an eternal home for you right by His side in heaven.

If that doesn't make you feel strong, what will?

Father, because You've adopted me, I know that I can be strong, no matter what comes. I look forward to my eternal home with You.

WHEN YOU TRIP

I forget everything that is behind me and look
forward to that which is ahead of me.
My eyes are on the crown.
PHILIPPIANS 3:13–14

Your legs and arms are pumping in rhythm, sweat is running from your forehead, your eyes are locked onto the finish line ahead. You're in first place when suddenly. . . you trip.

You sigh, slowly rising to your feet to stare at the tiny rock that messed you up. You wonder what the race would have been like if you hadn't fallen.

Perhaps you're thinking, *Just keep running! Standing there won't do anything!* It's what you do after a fall that matters.

The same is true in our walk with God. When we mess up, it's tempting just to stop and focus on the mistake. Meanwhile, life passes by—along with the good things God has promised.

Strong boys realize that a mistake isn't the end. It's just another starting point for a better finish.

God, I know I make mistakes. Teach me
to keep running whenever I trip.

FROM THE SIDELINES

Whatever work you do, do it with all your heart. Do it for the Lord and not for men.
COLOSSIANS 3:23

Have you ever been to a close basketball game? If so, you know how loud the crowd can get during the final moments. The entire gym erupts into cheers whenever the home team goes on offense.

As for the guy who has the ball? He *loves* it! The rush of hearing the crowd cheering him on makes him more determined than ever. He shoots, and the only thing going through his mind is, *This one's for the fans.*

Think about this: God is *your* biggest fan. Whenever you face a tough choice between right and wrong, He is cheering you on from the sidelines. He loves seeing you succeed, and He can't wait to celebrate with you after the game is over.

Next time you feel pressured to do wrong, let God's cheering give you strength. Straighten your backbone, line up your best shot, and think, *This one's for You, God.*

God, I want to make You happy with the choices I make. Thank You for all the support You give me each day.

NO MORE APPLES FOR YOU

*"I am the Vine and you are the branches. Get your
life from Me. Then I will live in you and you will
give much fruit. You can do nothing without Me."*
JOHN 15:5

Imagine you see a tree full of ripe apples and think, *I'd like
some of that.*

So you saw off a branch and take it home. Next year,
that branch will bloom again, and you'll have all the apples
you'd like, right?

Wrong. The moment you removed that branch from
the tree, you killed it. Once you eat the apples from that
dead branch, you're done. A branch that's not connected
to the rest of the plant is no good for anyone.

That's how Jesus describes our lives. If we stay connected to Him, we'll be strong and healthy and produce
"fruit"—love, joy, peace, and other great things (see Galatians 5:22–23). If we wander away from Him, we'll dry up,
die, and be pretty much useless.

The choice is ours. Let's make a good one!

---

*Help me stay connected to You, Jesus.
I never want to try growing fruit alone.*

ANCHORED AND SAFE

This hope is a safe anchor for
our souls. It will never move.
HEBREWS 6:19

Imagine if ships didn't have anchors. Whenever a storm came, they'd be tossed around like toys on the water. Before long, they'd be way off course.

That's pretty much what a life without God looks like.

Here on earth, the storms come up often—people we love get sick, kids at school treat us unkindly, and things we were hoping for just don't work out. Without an anchor, we'd be lost. Everything would feel hopeless, and our lives would just drift along.

That's where God steps in. When bad things happen, we can still be strong because we know He's leading us toward our final home with Him. You don't have to just drift around after a tragedy. Put up your sail of hope and push toward the goal.

Lord, I know You're the only anchor that can
withstand life's storms. Help me to rely on
You whenever I start drifting off course.

STURDY SHELTER

Lead me to the rock that is higher than I. For You have been a safe place for me. . . Let me live in Your tent forever. Let me be safe under the covering of Your wings.
PSALM 61:2–4

The hiker noticed the storm clouds a little too late.

He'd been roaming far from the campsite, collecting new plants and taking pictures of wildlife, when the first drop of rain told him trouble was coming. In the distance, he could see trees bending beneath the weight of a downpour, and it was coming his way.

He hurried down the mountainside as the wind picked up. Huge raindrops were pelting the ground. Finally, he reached safety—the sturdy, heavy-duty tent he'd paid good money for. No matter what was happening outside, he was safe and dry inside the shelter.

Be thankful that God is your strong and sturdy shelter. Never be afraid to hide in Him. He's the only safe place when the storm strikes.

In You, Lord, I know I can be strong and safe.
Thank You for protecting me from life's crazy storms.

THREE METHODS—ONE RESULT

"I will give you strength, and for sure I will help you. Yes, I will hold you up with My right hand that is right and good."
Isaiah 41:10

Today's verse promises us three things: strength, help, and a strong right hand to hold us up. But what does that look like in everyday life?

Well, imagine you're about to take a test. You've studied for days, but now the nervousness is starting to kick in. You pray, and you immediately feel calm and confident about what's ahead. That's strength.

As you're taking the test, you find yourself struggling with a few questions. Once again, you pray, and some of the answers come back to you. That's help.

When you're almost finished, a thought crosses your mind: *What if I cheat?* The smart kid is right next to you, after all—all it'd take is one peek. *No*, you decide. *I've got to do what's right.* That's God holding you up.

Today, thank God for coming to your rescue each day, even when you don't realize He's there.

Lord, I know You're by my side,
helping me in every way. Thank You.

OFF THE CHOPPING BLOCK

*Let us go with complete trust to the throne of God.
We will receive His loving-kindness and have His
loving-favor to help us whenever we need it.*
HEBREWS 4:16

In a classic book called *Alice in Wonderland*, the Queen of Hearts is a mean-tempered ruler with a nasty habit of yelling, "Off with their heads!" every time someone offends her. Not surprisingly, she wasn't very popular. Everyone was scared to death of her.

Today's verse reminds us that God is the exact opposite of the Queen of Hearts. He's a King who loves His people so much that He even took the punishment that we all deserved. He stepped *on* the chopping block so we could step *off*.

We don't have to be afraid when we approach God. No matter how badly we've messed up, we can come to Him for forgiveness. He is more than happy to give it to us.

---

*Thank You, God, for being so kind and merciful.
Give me the strength to come straight
to You whenever I mess up.*

ALL THE TIME IN THE WORLD

My times are in Your hands. Free me from the
hands of those who hate me, and from those who
try to hurt me. Make Your face shine upon Your
servant. Save me in Your loving-kindness.
PSALM 31:15–16

When you're talking about God's knowledge and power, it's impossible to exaggerate. For example, just look at part of today's scripture: "My times are in Your hands."

Not only is your happiness, your safety, and your life in His hands—your *time* is there too. Under God's care, time itself is a tool that He uses to accomplish His plan.

Wow! That kind of power can sound scary until you read the rest of the verse. You see, because God loves us, He uses His power to reward—not punish or frighten—the people who follow Him. He's plotted our lives from beginning to end, and what a happy ending it will be.

If you ever feel the pressure that you're running out of time, be strong: God's got all the time in the world.

Thank You, Father, for being so powerful.
I know I can trust You with every bit of my life.

LYING LIPS

Let the lying lips be quiet. For they speak with
pride and hate those who do right and good.
PSALM 31:18

Freddy hated how dull his life was. Everyone else seemed to enjoy fancy vacations, but the biggest thing Freddy could describe was a weekend camping trip.

So he came up with a plan: he'd just tell people he'd visited all kinds of amazing places. Sure, it was a lie, but who would notice?

Well, lots of people. Friends started poking holes in his stories. "Didn't I see you in town Saturday?" they would say. "How could you have been in Japan?"

Then Freddy told more lies to try to explain. Before long, hardly any of his friends wanted to be around him. Nobody believed him anymore. That's when Freddy realized something: people didn't want Freddy's stories, they wanted *Freddy*—the honest one.

He decided to apologize, and he learned a lesson as he did. Telling the truth was harder than ever, but so worth it. Over time, his friends began to trust him again.

Lord, help me to be strong enough to tell the truth,
even when I think nobody wants to hear it.

OLD BOSS, NEW BOSS

*If your sinful old self is the boss over your mind,
it leads to death. But if the Holy Spirit is the boss
over your mind, it leads to life and peace.*
ROMANS 8:6

Imagine you're all grown up. You have a terrible job. Your boss gives his workers nothing but splintery wooden chairs to sit in. Every day, he storms into the office and screams at everyone. Oh, and the pay is terrible too.

Now imagine you're offered another job. Your new boss is friendly and kind. He throws pizza parties every week. Everyone gets a custom-designed chair. And the pay? A million dollars a year.

That's a picture of people's spiritual lives. We're all born into sin—a cruel boss that promises nothing but death. But it's all they know so they're afraid to change. The truth is that the Holy Spirit is the perfect "boss"—one who helps us every day and promises eternal life with God.

So who's *your* boss?

---

*Lord, I want to choose You as my boss each day.
Give me the strength to refuse that old
boss whenever he comes calling.*

CANCELED PLANS

There are many plans in a man's heart,
but it is the Lord's plan that will stand.
PROVERBS 19:21

Have you ever been excited for a great vacation, only for it to not work out? Maybe someone got sick, the car broke down, or the flight got canceled. You and your family had planned the trip for months, but you had to move on. That just *stinks.*

But today's verse reminds us that our own plans never have the final say. They have to get God's approval.

Who knows? Maybe your car or plane would have crashed, and God was just protecting you. Maybe you needed to be home that week to help someone who needed a friend. Maybe the things you did when you *weren't* on vacation could start a chain of events that would create good things a hundred years from now.

Because God is so smart, it's impossible to understand why He does some things. But just trusting that He knows best should give us the strength to say, "Not my plans, God, but Yours."

I don't know best, God, so I'm giving all my plans
to You. I know You alone have the perfect plan.

STICKY SITUATION

The fear of man brings a trap, but he who
trusts in the Lord will be honored.
PROVERBS 29:25

Have you ever heard of the sundew plant? Its leaves are coated with sugary beads that attract insects. The bugs come in thinking they found a snack but soon find out *they're* on the menu. Unable to free their feet from the sticky leaves, the bugs can only struggle while the plant closes around them.

But bugs aren't the only creatures that risk getting trapped. People can too. You see, many people want nothing more than to please others. They're so scared of making someone upset that they refuse to speak the truth. This only creates a bad cycle of lying and hiding. Pretty soon, they're trapped in their own fear like a bug in a sundew plant.

It takes strength to stand up for what's right, especially when it's unpopular. But the truth will never lead you into a trap—the truth sets you free.

Lord, I don't want to be afraid of what
my friends say when I talk about You.
Please make me bold and confident in my faith.

THIEF

"The robber comes only to steal and to kill and to destroy. I came so they might have life, a great full life."
JOHN 10:10

Only someone whose home was broken into really knows how frustrating and scary that is. *How could he just take our stuff?* People think. *And what if it happens again? Will he hurt me this time?*

Regular thieves are scary enough. But there's one thief that's far more threatening: the devil. Satan is the biggest thief of all, and he's not just after our electronics. He wants something far more important: our souls.

Thankfully, this is where God's grace appears. Whenever you're following God, the devil simply can't get in. He's not allowed. He can knock and yell and jiggle the doorknob all he wants, but your soul is completely safe.

The only way the devil can get to you is if you let him. Don't.

Thank You, God, for protecting my soul with a "devil-proof" lock—Your salvation. Give me wisdom to recognize the devil's schemes and be strong enough to say no.

OPEN CURTAINS

This is what we heard Him tell us.
We are passing it on to you. God is light.
There is no darkness in Him.
1 JOHN 1:5

Did you know that darkness isn't really a thing by itself? Darkness is just the absence of light. That's why the two can't mix—wherever light is present, darkness can't exist.

Today's verse compares God to a beam of light. Whenever He's around, evil not only runs but simply goes out of existence altogether. So if we're living in God's will, the devil can't touch us. But if we start closing our spiritual curtains and blocking God out of our lives, it just gets darker and darker in our hearts. Pretty soon, we won't even be able to see where we're going. It gets harder and harder to find the curtains and open them again.

Strong boys make sure their hearts are always wide open for God's light to shine through. After all, who wants to live in the dark?

Keep my heart open to You, God. I want my
life to be bright with Your love so others
can see how wonderful You are.

FLIPPED AROUND

"You planned to do a bad thing to me. But God planned it for good, to make it happen that many people should be kept alive, as they are today."
GENESIS 50:20

Have you ever seen words written backward on a page? Many people have trouble trying to read them. But if you hold them up to a mirror, this confusing jumble of letters suddenly becomes a clear message.

God's plan for your life is like that mirror. Whenever people say and do hurtful things, life seems like a jumbled mess. Your brain hurts just thinking about it. *What's the purpose?* you may wonder.

But to God, all those jumbled pieces reflect His ultimate plan. Even if you can't see it right now, He's using every disappointment to one day flip the odds back in your favor. And one day, whenever you're in heaven with Him, you'll see the whole picture and say, "Thank You, God, for working everything out for good."

I know You're making good things out of bad situations, God. Give me the strength to keep believing that.

THE DARKEST VALLEY

Yes, even if I walk through the valley of the shadow of death, I will not be afraid of anything, because You are with me. You have a walking stick with which to guide and one with which to help. These comfort me.
PSALM 23:4

At some point, everyone has a "valley of the shadow of death" moment in life. You might see a loved one get sick or even die. You might get really sick yourself. Maybe it will be less severe but still very difficult—like the sadness of moving to a new town or hearing a friend say something nasty and hurtful to you.

The valley looks different for every person. But two things are certain: (1) it's never pleasant, and (2) God is always right there for His kids. He promises never to leave you (Deuteronomy 31:8), even when the shadows are closing in. His Holy Spirit will be your guide, telling you where to turn and what to do.

It doesn't matter how deep or dark the valley is. You can be strong knowing that God is your guide.

Guide me, Lord, to safety. I'm trusting You to show me the way.

143

WATCHING FOR GOD

*But as for me, I will watch for the Lord. I will wait
for the God Who saves me. My God will hear me.*
MICAH 7:7

It takes work to keep watching for good things. Our boredom, our fears, even our fun (like video games) can cause us to take our eyes off the important things of life.

That's why the writer of today's verse reminded himself of the importance of watching for God. As soon as Micah took his eyes off God—the God who could give him hope—trouble followed close behind. But as long as he kept looking for God, expecting Him to step in and help, Micah had hope. He could find the determination to press on.

Strong boys never take their eyes off God and His plan. They keep watching for the Lord, no matter what happens around them.

What are you watching today?

---

*God, it's so hard sometimes to keep my eyes on Your love,
especially when everyone and everything else is trying so
hard to grab my attention. Help me keep watching for You.*

SPIRITUAL WEIGHTLIFTING

We want you to know, Christian brothers, of the
trouble we had in the countries of Asia. The load was
so heavy we did not have the strength to keep going.
At times we did not think we could live. We thought
we would die. This happened so we would not put our
trust in ourselves, but in God Who raises the dead.
2 CORINTHIANS 1:8–9

Weightlifting is something that hardly anyone enjoys, but people do it anyway. Why? Because they know it will increase their strength. "No pain, no gain," as they say.

Today's scripture talks about spiritual weightlifting. Sometimes, God will give us a really heavy load. Even though He's carrying most of it Himself, the part He's given to us is often heavier than we think we can handle. But by stretching our spiritual muscles—by showing faith in the middle of the pain—we'll grow stronger. We'll strengthen our relationship with God.

Don't ever be afraid of weightlifting. It all pays off in the end.

Lord, thank You for stretching my spiritual
muscles. I want to grow in my walk with You.

THE SHARPEST SWORD OF ALL

*So give yourselves to God. Stand against
the devil and he will run away from you.*
JAMES 4:7

Wow, what a promise! But what does it mean? How can one boy stand against the biggest evil in the universe?

For the answer, look to Jesus. In Matthew 4, He'd been in the wilderness for forty days without food or water. That's when Satan came to Him and tempted Him three times. But each time, Jesus shot back with a verse of scripture. And what happened next? "The devil went away from Jesus" (Matthew 4:11).

Hebrews 4:12 says the Bible is "sharper than a sword that cuts both ways." Not only does it give us strength from day to day, but it also makes for a powerful weapon against Satan.

So how does one boy stand against the devil? By learning the Word of God and using it to cut right through the enemy's lies.

---

*God, teach me how to use Your Word to stand against
the devil. I don't want to be caught unprepared.*

STRENGTH VS. PEACE

The Lord will give strength to His people.
The Lord will give His people peace.
PSALM 29:11

Today's verse hints that strength and peace are two sides of the same coin. But how is that possible? Isn't strength mainly for *un*peaceful times—for battles and conflicts and storms?

Yes. And no. You see, the peace in this verse isn't something you see—it's a state of mind. The world around you can be as crazy and stressful as ever, but whenever God gives you the strength to trust in Him, you'll also have peace.

Imagine you're in a cement-block building constructed to withstand pretty much anything. That's the strength part. If a tornado comes when you're inside, you're not worried. That's peace.

No matter how unpeaceful life gets—when people and situations are just going crazy—you can have peace in your soul. Why? Because God is your strength.

Lord God, I'm so thankful for Your strength that
protects me and Your peace that comforts me.
Whenever I feel overwhelmed, help me to have both.

SHINE LIKE THE MOON

Jesus spoke to all the people, saying, "I am the Light of the world. Anyone who follows Me will not walk in darkness. He will have the Light of Life."
JOHN 8:12

You probably know that the moon doesn't give off its own light. It's just a big chunk of rock that reflects light from the sun. Though we can't see the sun at night, its beams still light up the moon's surface.

That's kind of how our faith works.

Worldly people can't see God right now. But they *can* see His light that bounces off our lives. When we choose to follow God in an ungodly world, His love and holiness shine like the moon to everyone who sees us.

Strong boys don't try to be flashlights. They know their light doesn't come from themselves. They just want to be good mirrors, bouncing God's light off their souls.

God, I want to reflect You to a world that needs Your light. Smooth out my rough spots so I can shine with the light of Your love.

UNCHANGING

"I am the First and the Last.
I am the beginning and the end."
REVELATION 22:13

Think back in time as far as you can. The day of your own birth? Go further. The ancient Egyptians? Go further. Back when dinosaurs walked the earth? Even *further*. What about the beginning of the universe? There you go. Now go back one more step to before anything existed. All you'd find is nothingness. . .and God.

Now think *forward*, all the way to the end of the world. Everything we know has been changed into something new. But God is still there.

That's right: God was there at the beginning, and He'll be there at the end. He's the only thing that hasn't changed and never will. So why should we worry about anything? To God, the future is no different from the present or the past. He's plotted it all out like a book. And if you love Him, He's already made sure your ending will be fantastic.

I'm so glad, Lord, that You never change. It gives me the strength to face all the things that do change.

CAN'T KEEP QUIET

The Lord is great and our praise to Him should be great.
He is too great for anyone to understand. Families of
this time will praise Your works to the families-to-come.
They will tell about Your powerful acts. I will think about
the shining-greatness of Your power and about Your
great works. Men will speak of Your powerful acts that
fill us with fear. And I will tell of Your greatness.
PSALM 145:3–6

It's hard to keep quiet about God when you really know Him. Today's scripture says that God's power is so great that His kids can't help passing it on.

Imagine if the king of England came to your house for dinner. After he left, would you never tell a soul? Or would you run through the streets, yelling, "I just met the king of England!"? Well, God is bigger and more important than a million kings of England put together. . .and He lives in your heart.

Today, be bold and tell people how great God truly is.

Lord, I'm amazed that You've decided to live in my
heart. Give me the courage to tell everyone I know.

PLUCKED-UP PLANTS

*As you have put your trust in Christ Jesus the Lord
to save you from the punishment of sin, now let Him
lead you in every step. Have your roots planted deep
in Christ. Grow in Him. Get your strength from Him.
Let Him make you strong in the faith as you have been
taught. Your life should be full of thanks to Him.*
COLOSSIANS 2:6-7

If you pull a plant from the ground, what happens? If you
don't quickly stick it in a vase with some water, it will
wither and die in no time. Plants need water to keep them
alive.

The same is true for our walk with God. Before we
met Him, we were like plants pulled up from the earth—
ready to die. But after we put our trust in Jesus Christ,
we received water in the form of His Word and a deep
relationship with Him.

To stay healthy and strong, stay connected to Jesus.
Let your roots reach deep into His living water.

---

*Help me, Lord, to keep my spiritual roots planted in Your
grace. I never want to wither like a plucked-up plant.*

SMARTER THAN AN ANT?

*"Agree with God, and be at peace
with Him. Then good will come to you."*
JOB 22:21

Imagine an ant trying to argue with a human. (First, you need to imagine that an ant can talk!) The human is telling the ant about how big the universe is—with its stars and galaxies and planets and solar systems. The ant, however, is having none of it.

"No," the ant says. "You've got it all wrong. The sun is just a few feet in the air, and its only purpose is to warm up my little anthill. Nothing else is out there."

What a funny little insect! But before you laugh at the ant for being foolish, think of all the times we act the same way toward God.

"No," we say to God. "You've got it all wrong. My life was supposed to go *this* way, and now You've messed it all up." But in reality, it's God who drew up the plans—all we can do is choose whether to follow along.

Lord, give me the wisdom and strength to agree with You, even when I don't understand what You're doing.

SHAKY KNEES

Then Nebuchadnezzar became very angry and called for Shadrach, Meshach, and Abed-nego. And they were brought to the king. Nebuchadnezzar said to them, "Is it true, Shadrach, Meshach and Abed-nego, that you do not serve my gods or worship the object of gold that I have set up? Now if you are ready to get down on your knees and worship the object I have made. . .very well. But if you will not worship, you will be thrown at once into the fire."
DANIEL 3:13–15

It takes a lot of strength to stand with shaky knees, especially when it will get you tossed into a blazing furnace.

But that's exactly what the three Hebrew boys did— and God took notice. He didn't stop them from the crazy king's punishment, but God did step into the fire right beside them to keep them from getting burned.

Today, don't be afraid of what people say about you. God's approval is worth standing up for.

Lord, when it's hard to stand for what's right, strengthen my legs. I know You can protect me from anything people throw my way.

A DIFFERENT KIND OF STRENGTH

"If we are thrown into the fire, our God Whom we serve
is able to save us from it. And He will save us from
your hand, O king. But even if He does not, we want
you to know, O king, that we will not serve your gods
or worship the object of gold that you have set up."
DANIEL 3:17–18

God wants us to stand up for Him. However, notice how the three Hebrew boys acted. They weren't rude. They didn't call attention to themselves or give a snarky speech on how ugly the king was. Instead, they just respectfully told the king that they refused to bow to his idol.

A lot of boys try to look "tough" in order to show their strength. But true strength doesn't cause a fuss—it says what needs to be said and leaves the rest to God. As a result, true strength looks a lot like love—because they both come from the same source.

That's the kind of strength people notice.

Lord, I know my strength stems from You, not myself.
May my words and actions match up with this truth.

EXTREME FORGIVENESS

Then they took him out of the city and threw stones
at him. The men who were throwing the stones laid
their coats down in front of a young man named Saul.
While they threw stones at Stephen, he prayed, "Lord
Jesus, receive my spirit." After that he fell on his knees
and cried out with a loud voice, "Lord, do not hold this
sin against them." When he had said this, he died.
ACTS 7:58–60

Today's scripture is an extreme example of loving and forgiving your enemies. Even as people were killing him, Stephen prayed for them.

When other kids say hurtful things to you, how do you respond? Do you lash out with an even meaner insult? Or do you pray that God would show kindness and mercy to that person?

Strong boys remember that "getting revenge" just means you sank to the bully's level. Instead, they take the higher path—the path of God's forgiveness.

Lord, I'm glad You've forgiven me for all the ways
I've sinned and hurt You. Please give me Your
forgiving heart toward people who mistreat me.

TO PLAN, OR NOT TO PLAN?

Jesus said to His followers, "Because of this, I say to you, do not worry about your life, what you are going to eat. Do not worry about your body, what you are going to wear. Life is worth more than food. The body is worth more than clothes."
LUKE 12:22–23

It seems there are two types of people in the world: (1) those who ignore today's scripture and worry about everything, and (2) those who take it too literally and never plan for anything.

But these verses don't tell us to just forget about the future. If we did, nothing would ever get done. Instead, they tell us not to let the future stress us out.

It's all right to plan. But sometimes, planning simply isn't an option—the future is a great big question mark. During these times, Jesus' words are the most useful. When our own plans fail, that's when it's time to sit back and watch *God's* plan play out.

Your future is in good hands.

Help me, God, not to worry about tomorrow, even when I have no plans. I know You'll provide for me, just like You always have.

EVERY DAY IS THANKSGIVING

Go into His gates giving thanks and into His holy place
with praise. Give thanks to Him. Honor His name.
PSALM 100:4

"Thanksgiving" isn't just for November. No, it's an attitude that God says you should have all year.

What are some ways you can give thanks? Well, the first and most obvious way is to tell God how grateful you are for all the good things you have. What things? How about His salvation, your family, your friends, your house . . .you name it.

But you can go even further by thanking God for things you don't yet have or the blessings you don't know about. After all, God is always working behind the scenes in your life. So your "blessings list" is kind of like an iceberg—all you can see is the tip.

And don't forget to tell God how thankful you are for *Him.* After all, the fact that He's always part of your life is the biggest blessing of all.

Lord, please grow my gratitude. I want to
see Your blessings everywhere I turn.

MERCY OVER FEAR

So Manoah said to his wife, "We will die for sure.
For we have seen God." But his wife said to him, "If the
Lord had wanted to kill us, He would not have received
a burnt gift and grain gift from us. He would not have
shown us all these things, or let us hear these things."
JUDGES 13:22–23

Manoah's wife—the mother of the strongman Samson—
made some really good points. As her husband jumped to
the worst possible conclusions, she reminded him: If God
had wanted to kill them, why would He have shown them
mercy?

Today, some people imagine God as an angry old man,
ready to zap anyone who steps out of line. When people
trip up and sin, they get scared. They believe they've
passed the point of no return. But that's when Jesus says,
If I wanted you dead, would I have died in your place?

Today, you can be strong in God's love. Remember
that no matter how badly you might have messed up,
you're just a prayer away from forgiveness.

Thank You, God, for wanting to show mercy to me.
Because of Your love, I know there's no reason to fear.

THE ONLY EXAMPLE THAT MATTERS

So the Lord said, "I will destroy man whom I have made from the land, man and animals, things that move upon the earth and birds of the sky. For I am sorry that I have made them." But Noah found favor in the eyes of the Lord. This is the story of Noah and his family. Noah was right with God. He was without blame in his time. Noah walked with God.
GENESIS 6:7–9

Do you ever feel like Noah?

Maybe all the kids around you love doing wrong—they say bad words, they make fun of others, they cheat and steal. You, on the other hand, know these things are wrong, so you refuse to go along.

That's exactly what happened to Noah. And guess what? God rewarded him. Because Noah chose to stand apart from the crowd by his choice, God made sure Noah wasn't part of the crowd when the floodwaters came.

Strong boys remember that God's example is the only one worth following.

Lord, help me to be strong enough to rise above the actions of others. I want to serve You, even when it's not popular.

GETTING YOUR FEET WET

*They carried it to the Jordan and put their feet in the
water. (For the Jordan water floods during the time of
gathering grain.) Then the water flowing down from
above stood and rose up in one place. . . The water
flowing down toward the sea of the Arabah, the Salt Sea,
was all cut off. So the people crossed beside Jericho.*
JOSHUA 3:15–16

God had promised His people that they could cross the
Jordan. The people in front—the priests—just had to step
into the water first.

That sounds easy enough, right? But the priests might
have been a little nervous. At this time, the Jordan was
flooded. It would almost certainly drown anyone who
plunged in. To step into its waters would have taken a lot
of faith.

But sometimes God calls all of us to be front-line
Christians—to obey Him even when it's scary. Even when
the idea seems crazy. As long as you trust His power and
love, you don't have to fear getting your feet wet.

---

*God, help me to be strong enough to take the
plunge, no matter what You call me to do.*

NO GIANT TOO BIG

*As he talked with them, Goliath the Philistine from
Gath came out of the army of the Philistines, and
spoke the same words as before. And David heard
him. When all the men of Israel saw the man, they
ran away from him and were very much afraid.*

1 SAMUEL 17:23–24

All of us have a Goliath. No, it may not be a gigantic man
staring down at you with a sword (at least, we *hope* that's
not the case!). Your Goliath can be any situation that
makes you feel small and afraid.

A test at school might be your Goliath. Maybe it's a
bully who won't leave you alone. Or maybe God wants you
to tell someone about Jesus, and your Goliath is fear.

Today's scripture gives a good example of how *not*
to react to a Goliath—by running away. After all, that just
pushes your problem farther down the road. Be strong,
knowing that even the tallest giant is no bigger than an ant
in the eyes of God.

*Thank You, Lord, for being strong for me
whenever I'm scared. I know that with You,
no giant is too big to conquer.*

THE BIG ONE

*David said to Saul, "Your servant was taking care of his
father's sheep. When a lion or a bear came and took a
lamb from the flock, I went after him and fought him
and saved it from his mouth. When he came against me,
I took hold of him by the hair of his head and hit him
and killed him. . . . And David said, "The Lord Who saved
me from the foot of the lion and from the foot of the
bear, will save me from the hand of this Philistine." Saul
said to David, "Go, and may the Lord be with you."*
1 SAMUEL 17:34–35, 37

David was an ordinary shepherd boy who was simply doing
his job. Whenever he fought wild animals, he had no idea
that these experiences were paving the way for his biggest challenge yet: Goliath.

But by learning to trust God through the trials that
came his way, David was able to stand strong whenever
"the big one" came.

---

*Lord God, help me to stand strong in each
tiny problem I face today. I want to trust
You in every situation, big or small.*

DRESSED TO WIN

Then Saul dressed David with his clothes. He put a brass head covering on his head, and dressed him with heavy battle-clothes. David put on his sword over his heavy battle-clothes and tried to walk, for he was not used to them. Then David said to Saul, "I cannot go with these, for I am not used to them." And David took them off.
1 SAMUEL 17:38–39

Christians are called each day to go out and fight the devil. But how can a person fight without armor?

Well, today's scripture shows that a godly warrior doesn't need a bunch of equipment to fight with—all he needs is *God's* armor (Ephesians 6:10–18). This spiritual protection includes the sword of the Spirit, the shield of faith, and the helmet of salvation. In a spiritual battle, the most important thing is keeping your heart, mind, and soul safe from the enemy's fiery arrows.

Strong boys don't walk into battle unprepared. They make sure they're dressed to win.

---

*Lord, I can't fight against Satan on my own.
Give me all the tools I need to hold my
own against his evil schemes.*

ODD METHODS

*David put his hand into his bag, took out a stone and
threw it, and hit the Philistine on his forehead. The stone
went into his forehead, so that he fell on his face to
the ground. . . . There was no sword in David's hand.*
1 SAMUEL 17:49–50

When you imagine a normal guy fighting a giant, what
goes through your mind? A movie-style battle with flash-
ing swords? Jumps and flips and twists? How about a single pebble slung into the giant's forehead?

God is never limited by our expectations. Though He
always comes through for His kids, it's rarely in the way
we'd expect. When David flung a small rock into Goliath's
exposed forehead, any doubt about the true winner was
erased. This victory belonged to *God*.

It takes faith to let God work in your life, especially
when His methods are odd. But odd methods are just
another way that God lets the world know who's really in
charge. He is what makes you strong.

---

*Lord, I want You to work in my life, no matter how
strange Your methods may seem. I never want to take
credit for something that only You could have done.*

LOVE—IT ISN'T EASY

"I say to you who hear Me, love those who work against you. Do good to those who hate you."
LUKE 6:27

"Loving your enemies" sounds like a great thing, doesn't it? You can find the idea in all kinds of movies, songs, books, and political speeches. It definitely has a ring to it.

So why is it *so hard*?

Loving your enemies isn't some warm, fuzzy feeling. It's a tough, tiring war that happens in our minds. When someone hurts our feelings, our natural instinct is to think, *How can I get even?* It feels like revenge will prove how strong we are. But in reality, *love* is the true sign of strength. After all, it takes God's power to fight against our human nature.

A strong boy doesn't say, "How can I make that person pay?" Strong boys say, "How can I repay that person with good?"

Thank You, Lord, for loving me, even when I don't deserve it. Teach me to show this love to everyone I know, even those who never show kindness in return.

AWKWARD OBEDIENCE

*Moses said to the Lord, "Lord, I am not a man of words.
I have never been. . . . For I am slow in talking and it
is difficult for me to speak." Then the Lord said to him,
"Who has made man's mouth?. . . Is it not I, the Lord?
So go now. . . . I will teach you what to say." But Moses
said, "O Lord, I ask of You, send some other person."*
EXODUS 4:10–13

Sometimes you'll feel like God is leading you to talk to
someone you'd rather avoid. You might think He's telling
you to make friends with that new kid who stays by himself. Or God is urging you to ask a friend about his relationship with God.

These feelings can be really awkward at first. Like
Moses, you might ask God, "Isn't there anyone else You
can send?" But God has a reason for picking *you*—and
the only way you'll discover that reason is if you trust and
obey Him.

---

*Father, please give me the strength to do
whatever You say even if it's awkward.
I want to be a part of Your great plan.*

GOD ISN'T FINISHED

*About three o'clock Jesus cried with a loud voice,
"My God, My God, why have You left Me alone?"*
MATTHEW 27:46

Today's scripture is one of the saddest verses in the whole Bible.

Many people have tried to understand exactly what Jesus meant by these words. Whatever the answer is, the point remains: Jesus felt totally abandoned by His Father.

If the Son of God could feel so sad, how are we any different? Sometimes we all feel like God has just walked away—like He no longer cares. It's one of the worst feelings in the world. But if you ever feel that way, look again at what happened to Jesus just three days later.

He rose from the dead! The Father wasn't finished with Him.

Whenever life gets you down—whether it's because of a sickness, a friendship that's falling apart, or even a tragedy—remember this truth: God isn't finished with you yet either.

---

*Thank You, Jesus, for enduring such an awful
experience for me. Remind me of Your example
whenever I feel like there's no hope.*

DON'T FORGET YOUR SWORD

Those who were building the wall and those who
carried loads did their work with one hand, and held
something to fight with in the other hand. Each
builder wore his sword at his side as he built.
NEHEMIAH 4:17–18

It can be hard to balance everyday life with your walk with God. Your homework and chores increase as you get older, and you want to spend more time with friends. With all of that happening, we're tempted to forget about God. But that can lead to disaster. After all, the enemy works best when we're distracted.

That's why God gives us His Word, which Ephesians 6:17 calls a sword—"the sword of the Spirit." God's Spirit stays by our side, leading us in the right direction according to what the Word says. We can go about our lives, ready at any moment to slice through the doubts and temptations that fly at us.

With God's Word and God's Spirit in your life, you'll be ready for anything.

Father, I never want to be caught off guard by the
devil's attacks. Train me to use the sword of Your Spirit,
and remind me to carry it with me wherever I go.

GROWLING LIONS

*"My God sent His angel and shut the lions' mouths.
They have not hurt me, because He knows that I am
not guilty, and because I have done nothing wrong to
you, O king." Then the king was very pleased and had
Daniel taken up out of the hole in the ground. So they
took Daniel out of the hole and saw that he had not
been hurt at all, because he had trusted in his God.*
DANIEL 6:22–23

Ever been to a zoo? If so, maybe you saw one of the scariest animals of all: the lion.

That big cat's teeth and claws are super sharp, so if you ever found yourself trapped by a lion. . .well, let's just say it wouldn't be pretty. Imagine how frightening it must have been for Daniel to be tossed into a den full of lions. Now imagine how happy he was when God shut their mouths.

That day, God proved His power over the "king of the jungle." He has power over anything and everything that can frighten us.

---

*Lord, I know You're able to rescue me from
any scary situation. Give me the strength
to trust You when I'm in a lion's den.*

NO HARM IN ASKING

Then Gideon said to God, "Do not let Your anger burn against me for speaking to You once again. Let me make one more test with the wool. Let it be dry only on the wool. And let the ground be wet all around it." God did so that night.

JUDGES 6:39–40

We all need reassurance sometimes. Sometimes we face a big decision, so we pray. And it's not sinful to wonder, *God, is that really You talking?* After all, our minds can play tricks on us.

Gideon asked God for two "signs," proof that he understood what the Lord wanted him to do. Some people think Gideon was wrong to do that, but God answered his requests. They showed just how seriously Gideon took God's commands. He wanted to make sure he got it right.

God won't always answer us with something we can touch or see. But He does often let us know through our hearts, through other people's words, and through "coincidences" that match up with our prayer.

If you're feeling unsure about God's calling, don't be afraid to ask.

Lord, I want to make sure I'm following You and not just my own imagination. Give me the wisdom to ask the right questions and the strength to obey when You answer.

GLASS HALF FULL

Then Caleb told the people in front of Moses to be quiet. And he said, "Let us go up at once and take the land. For we are well able to take it in battle." But the men who had gone up with him said, "We are not able to go against the people. They are too strong for us."
NUMBERS 13:30–31

Caleb was a "glass-half-full" kind of guy. He saw a challenge ahead and thought, *Wow, I can't wait to see what cool things God will do here!* The others saw the same challenge and thought, *Nope, too hard for me!*

What kind of boy are you? When you have a lot to do, do you think about how hard life is or do you take the plunge, excited to see how God will work things out?

A strong boy refuses to give in to a negative attitude. Instead, he chooses to be optimistic, even when everyone else says the glass is half empty.

I know that with You, God, the glass is always more than half full—it's filled to the brim. Thank You for giving me a reason for optimism.

IMPOSSIBLE. . .

*Then God said to Abraham, "As for Sarai your wife,
do not call her name Sarai. But Sarah will be her name.
And I will bring good to her. I will give you a son by
her. . . . Kings of many people will come from her." Then
Abraham fell on his face and laughed. He said to himself,
"Will a child be born to a man who is 100 years old?"*
GENESIS 17:15–17

How likely would it be for an ocean to split open and allow thousands of people to walk right through? It's impossible. . .but God did it.

What about an ordinary guy who's been dead for four days getting up and walking out of the grave? It's impossible. . .but God did it.

And how about a 100-year-old man having a child? Once again, it's impossible. . .but God did it.

See the pattern? God loves doing impossible things—it's just part of who He is. So the next time you feel like you're facing an impossible challenge, remember: *God can do it.*

---

*Lord, I know You're a God of the impossible. I can be
strong because I trust in You, the strongest of all.*

THE WAY GOD SPEAKS

*Joseph awoke from his sleep. He did what the angel of
the Lord told him to do. He took Mary as his wife.*
MATTHEW 1:24

Mary was about to have a baby, but she wasn't yet married. This was God's work, of course, but Joseph knew other people would think bad things. So he decided to break his engagement with Mary. That would save her some embarrassment.

But God had other plans.

Through a dream, an angel told Joseph to make Mary his wife. Confused but willing to obey God, Joseph agreed.

God may not speak to us through an angel. But He has other ways of getting our attention. He might use a godly friend's advice. He might give you a strong feeling that seems to come out of nowhere. He might allow situations to point you in a direction you wouldn't have chosen otherwise.

Strong boys are always watching and listening for God's direction, however it comes.

---

*Thank You, Lord, for choosing to guide
Your kids in the right direction. Help me
always to listen for Your instructions.*

DON'T OVERTHINK IT

Peter said to Jesus, "If it is You, Lord, tell me to come to You on the water." Jesus said, "Come!" Peter got out of the boat and walked on the water to Jesus. But when he saw the strong wind, he was afraid. He began to go down in the water.
MATTHEW 14:28–30

Have you ever done a really bad job at something you're really good at? Sometimes a good basketball player wants to impress someone in the stands, but then gets nervous and starts overthinking things. By focusing on his anxiety more than the game, he starts missing his shots.

Faith works sort of the same way. We do our best whenever we trust in God, refusing to get hung up on less important things (Think of Peter in today's scripture!) Whenever we focus on the waves instead of the Person who's allowing us to walk on them, we sink. When it comes to walking with God, the *who* is much more important than the *how*.

So when God asks you to do something, don't overthink it—just do it.

---

*Lord, strengthen my trust in You
so I can do the impossible.*

BIG MISTAKE

The Lord turned and looked at Peter. He remembered the Lord had said, "Before a rooster crows, you will say three times that you do not know Me." Peter went outside and cried with a troubled heart.
LUKE 22:61–62

Have you ever promised yourself that you wouldn't do something and then turned around and did exactly that? It feels terrible knowing you weren't strong enough to make the right decision—especially when you knew what you should do. In today's scripture, Peter found out just how awful that feeling is.

But there's good news. In John 21, Jesus—who had died on the cross, been buried, and then came back to life again—appeared to Peter. And guess what? He *forgave* Peter. Because Peter was truly sorry, Jesus allowed him to become one of the greatest men of God who ever lived.

The next time you fail like Peter did (and it will happen), tell God you're sorry. Then rejoice in His great forgiveness.

Help me to be strong enough to make the right choices, Father. But if I fail, give me even more strength to trust that You will forgive me.

WHEN HELPING IS HARD

*Now the God Who helps you not to give up and
gives you strength will help you think so you
can please each other as Christ Jesus did.*
ROMANS 15:5

Chance had been saving money for months to buy a new video game. He finally had enough, and he couldn't wait to go to the store after school. But as he walked across the playground toward home, he overheard some friends having a sad conversation.

"I can't get a new jacket," Isaac said. "My parents just don't have the money."

Chance suddenly noticed how chilly the wind was. And right then, that video game money felt like a big rock in his pocket. He'd been wanting that system for so long. But. . .

The game can wait, he told himself. *Someone needs this far more than I do.* Chance turned around said, "Hey, Isaac, do you have a minute?"

God, it's hard to put others before myself, but I know that's what You call me to do. Strengthen me so I can bless others, even if it means giving up something I want.

JOY = STRENGTH

*"Do not be sad for the joy of
the Lord is your strength."*
NEHEMIAH 8:10

What does the joy of the Lord look like in everyday life?
Does it mean laughing and smiling all the time, even in the
middle of tragedy? No, not at all.

God's joy is a natural response for the Christian whose
hope is in heaven. Think about it: if your future includes
a forever home with God, what can this life really do to
hurt you? No matter how bad things get, you know that
everything will work out perfectly in the end.

Sure, sad things will happen. It's okay to be sad when
they do. But don't stay there. The joy of the Lord should
motivate you to get up, wipe away any tears, and take the
next step in your walk with God.

---

*Lord, I want my strength to flow from the joy
You give me. Help me to remember that no
matter how sad I get, You have much better
things for me just around the corner.*

THE RIGHT REACTION

The woman left her water jar and went into the town. She said to the men, "Come and see a Man Who told me everything I ever did! Can this be the Christ?" They went out of town and came to Him.
JOHN 4:28–30

Many people call this person "the woman at the well." When Jesus told her that He was the Messiah, how did she respond? Did she say, "Huh," and then forget all about it? Did she brag about how special she was for the Savior to notice her?

No—she ran to tell others about how amazing *Jesus* was.

This woman had the perfect attitude about what was truly important. She knew how sinful she'd been, so she understood she couldn't take credit for anything good. But she also knew that what had happened was spectacular, so she couldn't stay quiet. She had to go tell someone.

When God blesses you, what's your reaction? Do you take it for granted, or do you give Him the praise He deserves?

I can't thank You enough, God, for blessing me and saving my soul. Help me always to point the praise back to You.

WHEN WEAK MEANS STRONG

*He gives strength to the weak. And He gives
power to him who has little strength.*
ISAIAH 40:29

When David defeated the giant Goliath, he was just an ordinary shepherd boy who couldn't even wear King Saul's armor.

When Moses went to Pharaoh with a message from God, he was just a normal guy who was afraid to talk in public.

When Saul first met Jesus, the man who would soon be called Paul was rounding up Christians to throw them in jail.

What do these guys have in common? None of them were "qualified" for their job. But God worked through them in fantastic ways. In fact, the weaker a person is, the more likely that person is to be picked by God.

Why? Because God loves to show that *His* power is at work, not anyone else's. When weak people do amazing things, it's easy to see God working behind the scenes.

The next time you feel weak, God might be preparing you to do something really powerful.

---

*God, I know I'm not able to do the work You've called
me to. That's why I'm trusting in You for strength.*

A DANGEROUS SPORT

Watch and keep awake! Stand true to the Lord.
Keep on acting like men and be strong.
1 CORINTHIANS 16:13

Have you ever watched boxing? If so, you know how alert the fighters have to be every second of each round. One small distraction means getting smashed in the face.

That's the kind of focus today's scripture says we should have in our walk with God. Our opponent, Satan, will throw everything he's got at us—lies, temptations, frustrations, doubts, you name it. Even worse, he never fights fair. He loves hitting below the belt.

How can we protect ourselves? The Bible offers many techniques: prayer, meditation on God, Bible study, and love. The more we learn these strategies, the better we'll hold up when we're in the ring.

Don't let the devil smack you around. With God's help, you can swat away his punches—and surprise him with a few shots of your own.

Lord, I want to stand my ground against the devil.
Teach me to study and apply Your Word.

HUMILITY WINS

Then Mary said, "I am willing to be used of the
Lord. Let it happen to me as you have said."
Then the angel went away from her.
LUKE 1:38

Pride stinks. You probably know that by now, but you might not know just how bad it can be.

Proud people want to act like every good thing is *their* idea. They hate the thought of being used by a higher power. To them, humility is a weakness. But God can't use proud people, so they're never able to accomplish all the great things He'd like them to.

Humble people, however, say to God, "You know best, so I'm willing to go along with whatever plans You have for me." These are the kind of people who make history—some we're still talking about hundreds of years later. Why? Because their plans aren't really theirs: they come straight from the mind of God.

Which kind of person do you choose to be?

Give me the strength and humility to choose
Your goals over my own, God. Use me for
whatever purpose You have planned.

STRENGTH IN NUMBERS

Elijah said. . . ."The people of Israel have turned away
from Your agreement. . . . Only I am left, and they
want to kill me." . . . [God said,] "I will leave 7,000
in Israel whose knees have not bowed down in front
of Baal and whose mouths have not kissed him."
1 Kings 19:10, 18

Imagine that you're in a play. You have two important scenes, but when your time comes to speak, you accidentally say the lines from your *second* appearance. Ugh! Every eye in the theater is on you, and you feel each one of them.

Sometimes, doing the *right* thing can feel like that. When everybody else is disobeying God's instructions, it feels awkward to be the only person who's actually following the rules.

But as He reminded Elijah in today's scripture, God makes sure that none of His kids are truly alone. Even if we don't know them, there are plenty of other faithful Christians in the world. And finding these people and developing friendships with them can strengthen us in our own walk with God.

God, whenever I feel like I'm the only one following You,
lead me to other Christians who are doing the same.

GODLY INFLUENCES

I remember your true faith. It is the same faith your grandmother Lois had and your mother Eunice had. I am sure you have that same faith also.
2 TIMOTHY 1:5

Which adults are a good influence in your Christian life? Maybe it's your parents who take you to church each Sunday. Maybe it's a grandparent who teaches you about the Bible. Or perhaps it's a Christian neighbor who spends quality time with you.

No matter who it is, be sure to thank God for that person. And make sure to tell him or her how grateful you are too. As Paul reminded Timothy in today's verse, the Christian teaching you receive when you're young will stick with you for your entire life. As you grow older, you'll have even more appreciation toward whoever taught you about the good news of Jesus.

Strong boys never forget the people God has used to grow their strength.

Thank You, Jesus, for sending someone to teach me about You. Help me never to take that person for granted or walk away from the lessons he's taught.

JAIRUS' REQUEST

Jairus was one of the leaders of the Jewish place of worship. As Jairus came to Jesus, he got down at His feet. He cried out to Jesus and said, "My little daughter is almost dead. Come and put Your hand on her that she may be healed and live."

MARK 5:22–23

Jairus' story has a double plot twist. When Jesus finally arrives at the man's house, his daughter is dead. What a depressing ending!

Except it isn't the end. To Jesus, death is no problem. He walks in, takes the twelve-year-old by the hand, and says, "Little girl, I say to you, get up!" (verse 41). Suddenly, her eyes flutter open, she gets up, and walks.

Just think: if Jairus wouldn't have been humble enough to ask Jesus for help, this amazing story would never have happened. But Jairus did ask, and Jesus gave him far more than he could have expected.

What can you ask God for today?

Lord God, I never want to miss out on Your blessings by refusing to ask. Remind me to pray each time I have a need.

DON'T BE CYNICAL

A woman came with a jar of perfume. She had given much money for this. As Jesus ate, she poured the perfume on His head. When the followers saw it, they were angry. They said, "Why was this wasted? This perfume could have been sold for much money and given to poor people." Jesus. . .said to them, "Why are you giving this woman trouble? She has done a good thing to Me."
MATTHEW 26:7–10

Jesus' disciples were learning how to think like Jesus. But today's scripture proves they still had a lot of work to do.

Instead of being happy that this woman was showing so much love to Jesus, they grumbled about a waste of money. Something beautiful was happening before their eyes, but they were *cynical*—suspicious and bitter and unkind.

Don't be like that. Look for God's blessings, even if you find them in unusual situations. Being cynical is easy, but God calls you to a better path.

Lord, give me spiritual eyes to replace any cynical thoughts I might have.

SHE STARTED IT!

The man said, "The woman whom You gave to be with me, she gave me fruit of the tree, and I ate."
GENESIS 3:12

What happens when kids get into a fight? Often times, a parent or a teacher or some other adult steps in to stop it. Then the kids point at each other and yell, "He started it!"

That's pretty much what Adam did in today's verse. God had told him and Eve not to eat the fruit of a certain tree, but they did it anyway. Eve was first to take a bite, and when she offered it to Adam, he ate too. So who was to blame?

Both of them were. Just because Eve "started it" doesn't mean Adam got off the hook. He had his own choice to make, and he chose poorly.

Whenever you make a mistake, don't be like Adam. Never try to shift the blame to someone else. Own up to your sin, ask for forgiveness. . .and thank God for His willingness to welcome you back.

I don't want to play the blame game, Lord.
Give me the strength to admit my mistakes.

RIGHT ON TIME

*Sarah was able to have a child and she gave birth
to a son when Abraham was very old. He was born
at the time the Lord said it would happen.*
GENESIS 21:2

When God told Abraham that his wife was going to have a
baby, his first thought was probably, *Um, isn't it a little too
late for that, God? I'm a hundred years old!*

But God works on His own schedule. If He says something will happen, it will happen, just as He said, even if it
seems late or impossible to us.

This is great news, especially when we just can't see
the purpose in what's happening around us. We may think,
*Lord, I know You said everything will work out for good but
isn't it a little late for that now?* During those times, just
hang on a little longer. You'll see (just like Abraham did)
that God is always right on time.

*Thank You, Lord, for being so dependable. Give me
the strength to be patient, even when I feel like You
should've acted long ago. I know Your timing is best.*

BURNED OUT

*Jacob loved Rachel. So he said, "I will serve you
seven years for your younger daughter Rachel." . . .
So Jacob worked seven years for Rachel. It was only
like a few days to him, because of his love for her.*
GENESIS 29:18–20

Have you ever gotten burned out on a job? Maybe it was
a school project. Maybe it was a big lawn that needed
mowed. Maybe it was a thousand-piece puzzle you were
putting together! The work was exciting at first, but over
time you started to lose interest.

Why is that? Maybe you forgot *why* you were doing
it. You originally wanted to please your teacher or make
some money or just relax and have fun. . .but you got distracted and frustrated.

It can be tough to keep working, even when we're
working for God. But He wants us to stay focused on
the end result: our eternal life with Him. That way, even
the hardest work will seem like only "a few days" once it's
all over.

---

*Help me always to finish what I start, God.
I know the reward will be worth it.*

A BRILLIANT PLAN

*She was going to have a baby, and she gave birth to a
son. When she saw that he was beautiful, she hid him
for three months. But the time came when she could
hide him no longer. So she took a basket made from
grass, and covered it with tar and put the child in it.
And she set it in the grass by the side of the Nile.*

EXODUS 2:2–3

When Moses' mother heard the rule that all the Hebrew
baby boys were to be killed, she was horrified. How could
Pharaoh say that?

But then she had an idea: "I don't have to let him die.
My baby will live, no matter what."

Talk about determination. She openly disobeyed Pharaoh's evil command with a brilliant plan to save baby
Moses' life. With God's help, the plan worked.

Don't you think God Himself was behind that plan?
You can imagine that Moses' mom had prayed and begged
God for His help. Some situations seem impossible, and to
us they are. But nothing is impossible for God.

---

*God, strengthen my determination to carry out
Your plan, even when it seems as if all hope is lost.*

THE WAY TO SUCCESS

*So the people called out and the religious leaders blew
the horns. When the people heard the sound of the horns,
they called out even louder. And the wall fell to the
ground. All the people went straight in and took the city.*
JOSHUA 6:20

Sometimes, God calls us to fight some pretty tough battles. He promises to be with us, of course, but He still expects us to show up and fight.

But there are times, as in today's scripture, that God tells us to sit back and watch.

There was no way the Israelites' army could get through Jericho's big, thick walls. So what did God do? He gave the people a crazy plan and took the wall down for them.

That day, there was no doubt that God had fought the battle for Israel. All the people had to do was obey, and God took care of the rest.

Knowing that God fights battles for you is an amazing source of strength.

---

*God, please help me to obey You today and
all the days to come. I know You are strong
enough to pave my way to success.*